HEADWAY

STUDENT'S BOOK   PART A   UNITS 1–8   ELEMENTARY

Liz & John Soars

Oxford University Press 1996

STUDENT'S BOOK

WORKBOOK

UNIT 1

***am/is/are* – Possessive adjectives – Spelling**

Hello!

PRESENTATION (1)

T 1a Read and listen.

A Hello. My name's Jenny. What's your name?
B Anna.
A Where are you from, Anna?
B I'm from New York.

> ⚠️
>
> name's = name is
> what's = what is
> I'm = I am

Practice

1 Writing and listening

Complete the conversation.

A Hello. My _____ Thomas.

   What's _____ name?

B Johann.

A _____ are you from, Johann?

B _____ from Berlin.

   Where _____ you from?

A _____ _____ Oxford.

T 1b Listen and check.

2 Speaking

Stand up!
Talk to the students in the class.

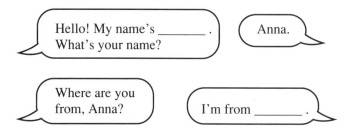

> Hello! My name's _____ .
> What's your name?

> Anna.

> Where are you from, Anna?

> I'm from _____ .

PRESENTATION (2)

Read about Manuel.

My name's Manuel Garcia and I'm a doctor. I'm thirty. I'm married and I have two children. I live in a house in Seville in the south of Spain. I want to learn English for my job.

Practice

1 Writing and listening

Complete the text about Mayumi.

My name's Mayumi Kimura and I'm _____ **student.** I _____ nineteen years old. I'm not married. I have two brothers and a _____ . I _____ in a flat in Osaka, Japan. I _____ to learn English because it's an international _____ .

T2 Listen and check.

2 Writing and speaking

Write about you. Then read it to the class.

PRESENTATION (3)

1 **T3** Look at the stress marks. Practise saying the countries.

	●●	●●	●●●
France	England	Brazil	Germany
Spain	Egypt	Japan	Mexico
Greece	Russia		Hungary
			Italy

2 Look at the photographs and read the words.

¡Buenos días!

**This is Manuel.
He's from Spain.**

Konnichiwa!

**This is Mayumi.
She's from Japan.**

Hello!
Hello!

**This is Mike and Rosie.
They're from England.**

He's = He is
They're = They are

3 Write where the people are from. Choose one of the countries in Exercise 1.

Bonjour!

This is Jean-Paul.

_____

Guten Tag!

This is Johann.

_____

Salem ala goum!

This is Fatima.

_____

Buongiorno!

This is Paola.

_____

Hairetai!

This is Christina.

_____

Bom dia!
Bom dia!

This is Clara and Bruno.

_____

Privjet!

This is Ivan.

_____

¡Buenos días!

This is Pablo.

_____

Szia!
Szia!

This is János and Irén.

_____

Practice

1 Speaking

1 Work in pairs.
Ask and answer questions about the people in the photographs.

What's his name? — Manuel.

Where's he from? — Spain.

What's her name? — Mayumi.

Where's she from? — Japan.

2 Ask and answer the same questions about the students in the class.

2 Listening and pronunciation

T4 Tick (✔) the sentence you hear.

1 a She's from Spain.
  b He's from Spain.
2 a I'm sixteen.
  b I'm sixty.
3 a His name's Pat.
  b Her name's Pat.
4 a They're from Britain.
  b They're from Brazil.
5 a Where's she from?
  b Where's he from?
6 a He's a teacher in France.
  b His teacher in France.

3 Grammar

Put *am*, *is*, *are*, *his*, or *her* into the gaps.

Example
My name _is_ Anna.

a Where _____ you from?

b I _____ from Italy.

c 'What's _____ name?' 'Peter.'

d Christina _____ twenty-nine years old.

e Mike and Rosie _____ from London.

f Clara _____ married.

g 'What's _____ name?' 'Mayumi.'

h He _____ a doctor.

i I have a daughter. _____ name's Kate.

j János and Irén _____ married. They have a son.

4 Choosing the correct sentence

One sentence has a mistake. Choose the correct sentence.
Put ✔ and ✘.

Examples
His from Greece. ✘   She's a teacher. ✔
He's from Greece. ✔   She's teacher. ✘

1 a Where she from?   6 a I have two sisters.
  b Where's she from?   b I have two sister.
2 a What's her name?   7 a They from Japan.
  b What's she's name?   b They're from Japan.
3 a I'm a student.   8 a He's a doctor.
  b I'm student.   b His a doctor.
4 a She is twenty-nine   9 a He's name's Bruno.
    years old.   b His name's Bruno.
  b She has twenty-nine   10 a Her surname is
    years old.   Smith.
5 a I live in flat.   b Her surname it's
  b I live in a flat.   Smith.

● LISTENING AND SPEAKING

Hello and goodbye

1 Write the conversations in the correct order.

a Fine, thank you. And you?
   I'm OK, thanks.
   Hello, Mary. How are you?

   A _____

   B _____

   A _____

b Not bad, thanks. And you?
   Very well. How are the
     children?
   Hi, Dave! How are you?
   They're fine.

   A _____

   B _____

   A _____

   B _____

c Goodbye, Anne. Have a
     nice evening.
   Thanks, Chris. See you
     tomorrow!
   Goodbye, Chris.

   A _____

   B _____

   A _____

T5 Listen and check.

2 Stand up! Have conversations with other students.

10

● VOCABULARY AND PRONUNCIATION

1 Using a bilingual dictionary

Look at the extract from the *Oxford Italian Minidictionary*.

the word in English   the part of speech
                                (*n.* = noun)

apple /æpl/ *n.* mela *f.*

the pronunciation   the word in Italian

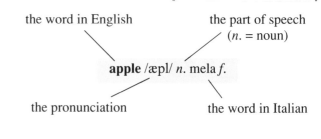

a

b

e

f

i

j

m

n

2 What's this in English?

1 Use your dictionary and match a word in the box with an object in the photographs.

Example
a *It's a dictionary.*

	● ●	● ● ●	● ● ●
a stamp a bag a map a key	an apple a postcard a ticket a notebook an orange a letter a suitcase a camera	a dictionary an envelope a newspaper	a magazine

2 **T6** Look at the stress marks (● ●). Listen and practise saying the words.

3 Look at the words.

an apple	*an* envelope
an orange	*a* bag
a ticket	*an* English book

When is it *a*? When is it *an*?

What are the letters *a*, *e*, *i*, *o*, and *u*?

3 A vocabulary notebook

Buy a notebook and write the new words in it. Translate the words.
This is an Italian student's notebook. Look at how she writes the stress marks.

● EVERYDAY ENGLISH

Spelling

1 **T 7a** Listen to the letters of the alphabet.
   Practise saying them.

   /eɪ/   a h j k
   /i:/   b c d e g p t v
   /e/   f l m n s x z
   /aɪ/   i y
   /əʊ/   o
   /u:/   q u w
   /ɑ:/   r

2 **T 7b** Listen to the alphabet song. Sing it!

3 **T 7c** Listen and write the words you hear.

4 **T 7d** Read and listen to the conversation.

   A How do you spell your first name?
   B J - A - M - E - S.
   A How do you spell your surname?
   B H - A - double R - I - S - O - N.
   A James Harrison.
   B That's right.

   In pairs, ask the same questions. Write the answers.

   (How do you spell your first name?)

   (How do you spell your surname?)

5 Ask and answer questions about things in the room.

   (What's this in English?) (A dictionary.)

   (How do you spell it?) (D-I-C-T-I-O-N-A-R-Y.)

   (What's this in English?) (I don't know.)

12

GRAMMAR SUMMARY

Verb *to be*

Positive

I	am	
He She It	is	from England.
We You They	are	

I'm   = I am
He's   = He is
She's = She is
It's   = It is
We're = We are
You're = You are
They're = They are

Question

	am	I	
Where	is	he she it	from?
	are	we you they	

I'm 20

I'm 20.   NOT ~~I'm 20 years.~~
I'm 20 years old.   ~~I have 20 years.~~

Possessive adjectives

What's	my your his her	name?
This is	its our your their	house.

What's = What is

a/an

It's a	ticket. dictionary. magazine.

We use *an* before a vowel.

It's an	apple. envelope. English dictionary.

Prepositions

Where are you **from**?
I live **in** a flat **in** Paris.
What's this **in** English?

Study the Word List for this unit on page 123.

UNIT 2

Questions and negatives – Possessive *'s* – Prices – *Can I have ...?*

People

PRESENTATION (1)

Questions and negatives

1 **T8** Write the numbers and phone numbers you hear.

2 Read about Mary Hopkins.

SURNAME	HOPKINS
FIRST NAME	MARY
COUNTRY	England
JOB	Journalist
ADDRESS	35, North Street, Bristol
PHONE NUMBER	0272 478 2209
AGE	23
MARRIED?	No

3 Complete the questions.

a What's **her** surname?   Hopkins.

b _____ her first name?   Mary.

c _____ she _____ ?   England.

d _____ _____ job ?   She's a journalist.

e What's _____ _____ ?   35 North Street, Bristol.

f _____ _____ phone number?   0272 478 2209.

g How old _____ _____ ?   Twenty-three.

h Is she _____ ?   No, she isn't.

T9 Listen and check. Practise saying the questions and answers.

4 Ask your teacher questions about Mary's brother.

> What's his first name?

Practice

1 Speaking

1 Student A   Look at the information on this page.
    Student B   Look at the information from your teacher.

Ask and answer questions to complete the information.

SURNAME	PETERS
FIRST NAME	
COUNTRY	Scotland
JOB	
ADDRESS	62, Church Street, Glasgow
PHONE NUMBER	
AGE	47
MARRIED?	

2 Ask your teacher the same questions.

> What's your name?

> Rosa Gonzalez.

> Are you married?

> Yes, I am./No, I'm not.

3 Look at the form from your teacher. Stand up! Ask two other students questions to complete the form about them. Answer questions about you.

4 Tell the class about one of the students.

> Her name's Anne-Marie. She's from Strasbourg.

13

2 Negatives and short answers

⚠️

1 Look at the negative forms.
    She **isn't** married.
    You **aren't** English.
But: I**'m not** a doctor.   NOT ~~I amn't~~ a doctor.

2 Look at the short answers to Yes/No questions.
    Is Mary English?   **Yes, she is.** (she = Mary)
    Is her surname Atkins? **No, it isn't.** (it = surname)
    Are you a doctor?   **No, I'm not.**

1 Ask and answer Yes/No questions about Mary and Martin.

About Mary

Example
French? German? English?

Is she French?   No, she isn't.

Is she German?   No, she isn't.

Is she English?   Yes, she is.

a a doctor? a teacher? a journalist?
b eighteen? twenty-one? twenty-three?

About Martin

c Smith? Jones? Peters?
d American? English? Scottish?
e a taxi driver? a shop assistant? a policeman?

2 Ask Yes/No questions about the students in the class.

Juan, are you married?   No, I'm not.

Is Maria a student?   Yes, she is.

3 Grammar

Make true sentences!

a We _____ in class.

b It _____ Monday today.

c I _____ at home.

d The teacher's name _____ David.

e My parents _____ at work.

f I _____ married.

g Champagne _____ a drink from Portugal.

h Egypt and Morocco _____ in Europe. They _____
   in Africa.

14

PRESENTATION (2)

Possessive *'s*

T 10 Look at the photograph of Martin Peters with his
family. Read and listen to the text. Write the names of the
people in the correct places.

This is a photo of Martin, his wife, and his children.
His wife's name is Jennifer. She's a dentist. His
daughter's name is Alison. She's twenty-three
and she's a hairdresser. His son's name is Andy.
He's nineteen and he's a student. Alison's boyfriend is a
travel agent. His name is Joe.

⚠️

His wife**'s** name   **'s** = possession. It is *not* the short
                              form of *is*.
                           His wife**'s** name = her name
She**'s** a dentist.   She**'s** = She is. *Is* is part of the
                              verb *to be*.

● Grammar question

Find other examples in the text of *'s* = possession, and *'s* = *is*.

Practice

1 Speaking

1 Ask and answer questions about Martin's family.

> Who's Jennifer?

> She's Martin's wife.

2 Ask your teacher questions about the names of his/her family.

> What's your mother's name?

> What's your sister's name?

2 Vocabulary

Use your dictionary and fill in the gaps.

husband	*wife*
son	
father	
	sister
uncle	
	niece
grandfather	

3 Speaking

Write down the names of some of the people in your family. Work in pairs. Ask your partner questions about his/her family.

> Who's Juan?

> He's my brother.

> Who's Sylvie?

> She's my aunt. She's my mother's sister.

4 Choosing the correct sentence

One sentence has a mistake. Choose the correct sentence. Put ✔ and ✘.

1　a　He's a engineer.
　　b　He's an engineer.
2　a　I'm a hairdresser.
　　b　I'm hairdresser.
3　a　I have twenty-one years old.
　　b　I am twenty-one years old.
4　a　My sister's name is Carmen.
　　b　My sisters name is Carmen.
5　a　She isn't married.
　　b　She no married.
6　a　I have two brothers.
　　b　I have two brother.
7　a　Where Wolfgang from?
　　b　Where's Wolfgang from?
8　a　That's Peter's book.
　　b　That's the book of Peter.

● VOCABULARY

Adjectives

1 Use your dictionary and match the opposites.

Example
old – young

difficult	horrible	lovely	easy
expensive	cold	small	right
old	cheap	old	young
hot	new	big	wrong

2 Write a sentence for each picture, using a word from Exercise 1.

a　*It's big.*　　　　　b　*It's small.*

c　　　　　　　　　　d

e　　　　　　　　　　f

g　　　　　　　　　　h

i　　　　　　　　　　j

k　　　　　　　　　　l

m　　　　　　　　　　n

o　　　　　　　　　　p

T11 Listen and check. Practise saying the sentences.

15

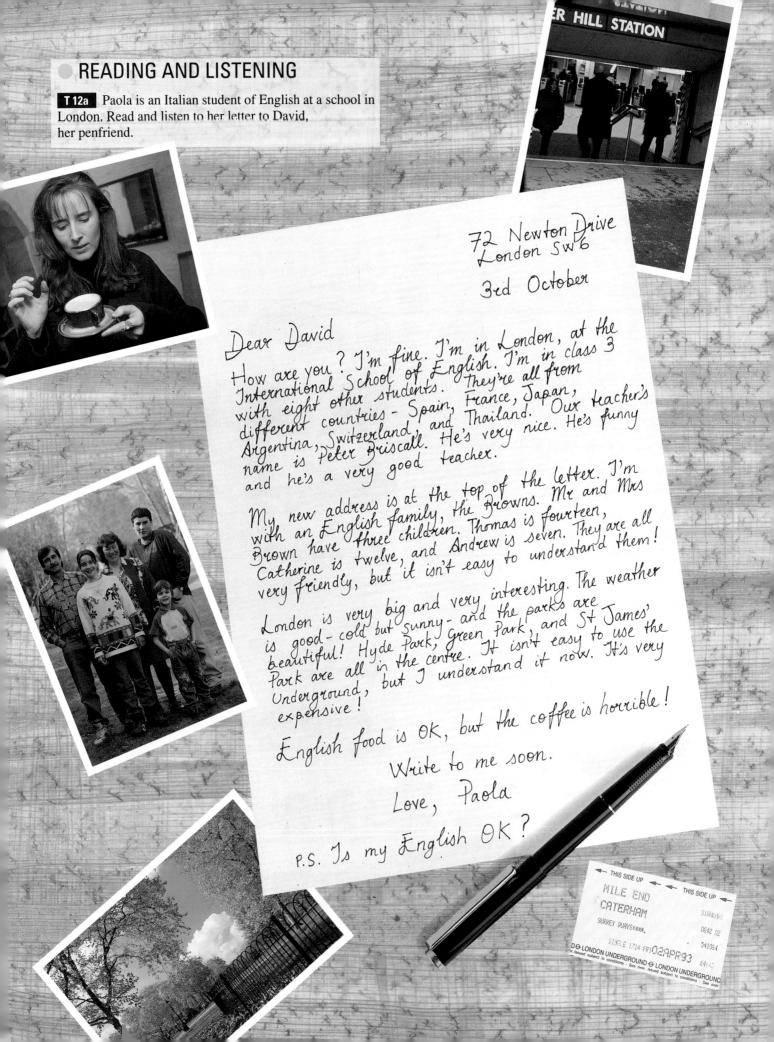

● READING AND LISTENING

T 12a Paola is an Italian student of English at a school in London. Read and listen to her letter to David, her penfriend.

72 Newton Drive
London SW6

3rd October

Dear David

How are you? I'm fine. I'm in London, at the International School of English. I'm in class 3 with eight other students. They're all from different countries — Spain, France, Japan, Argentina, Switzerland, and Thailand. Our teacher's name is Peter Briscall. He's very nice. He's funny and he's a very good teacher.

My new address is at the top of the letter. I'm with an English family, the Browns. Mr and Mrs Brown have three children. Thomas is fourteen, Catherine is twelve, and Andrew is seven. They are all very friendly, but it isn't easy to understand them!

London is very big and very interesting. The weather is good — cold but sunny — and the parks are beautiful! Hyde Park, Green Park, and St James' Park are all in the centre. It isn't easy to use the Underground, but I understand it now. It's very expensive!

English food is OK, but the coffee is horrible!

Write to me soon.

Love, Paola

P.S. Is my English OK?

Comprehension check

1 Match a picture with a part of the letter.

2 Are the sentences true (✔) or false (✘)?

Examples

Paola is Italian. ✔

She's in Rome. ✘ *No, she isn't. She's in London.*

a Paola's happy in London.
b She's on holiday.
c It's a very big class.
d The students in her class are all from Europe.
e Mr and Mrs Brown have two sons and a daughter.
f The Underground is cheap.
g The food in London is horrible.

3 Here are the answers to some questions about Paola's letter. Write the questions.

Example

Where's she from?
Italy.

a _____ ?
   Spain, France, Japan, Argentina, Switzerland, and
   Thailand.

b _____ ?
   Peter Briscall.

c _____ ?
   Fourteen.

d _____ ?
   Yes, it is. Cold but sunny.

e _____ _____ ?
   No, it isn't. It's horrible.

4 **T 12b** Listen to five conversation .ola has in London. Who is she with? Where is she?

Writing

Write a similar letter to a friend about your class.

● EVERYDAY ENGLISH

In a café

1 Look at the menu. Check the meaning of new words in your dictionary.

2 **T 13a** Listen and repeat.

3 Ask and answer questions.

> How much is a tuna sandwich?

> One pound seventy.

> How much is a chicken sandwich and a mineral water?

> Two pounds eighty.

4 **T 13b** Listen to the conversations and complete them.

a A Hello.

  B Hello. Can I have a

    _____ _____,

    please?

  A Here you are.

    Anything else?

  B No, thanks.

  A One pound _____,

    please.

  B Thanks.

  A Thank you.

b A Hi.

  B Hello. Can I have a

    cheese sandwich,

    please?

  A Anything to drink?

  B Yes. A _____

    _____ _____,

    please.

  A OK. Here you are.

  B _____ _____ is

    that?

  A One pound eighty,

    please.

  B Thanks.

c A Good morning.

  B Morning.

  A _____ _____

    _____ a hamburger

    and a cup of

    coffee, please?

  B OK. _____

    _____ _____.

  A Thanks. How much is

    that?

  B _____ _____

    twenty.

  A One, two, three

    pounds ... twenty p.

  B Thanks.

  A Thank you.

5 Work in pairs. Practise the conversations, then make
more conversations. Use real British money if you can!

18

GRAMMAR SUMMARY

Verb *to be*

Questions with question words   **Answers**

What	is her surname? is his job? is her address?		Lucas. He's a policeman. 34, Church Street.
Where	is she are you are they	from?	Portugal.
Who	is Jennifer? is she?		She's John's daughter.
How old	is he? are you?		Twenty-two.
How much	is a Coke?		Sixty pence.

Yes/No questions   **Short answers**

Is	he she it	hot?	Yes, he is. No, she isn't. Yes, it is.
Are	you they	married?	No, I'm not./No, we aren't. Yes, they are.

Negative

I	am			I'm not = I am not (I amn't)
He She It	is	not	from the States.	He isn't = He is not She isn't = She is not It isn't = It is not
We You They	are			We aren't = We are not You aren't = You are not They aren't = They are not

Possessive *'s*

My husband**'s** name is Martin.
That's Andrea**'s** dictionary.

Prepositions

I'm **in** London. I'm **in** class 3 **with** eight other students.
Green Park is **in** the centre.

I'm **at** home. My parents are **at** work.
I'm **at** the International School **of** Languages.

She isn't **on** holiday.
This is a photo **of** my family.

Study the Word List for this unit on page 123.

UNIT 3

Present Simple (1) – *What time is it?*

Work

PRESENTATION (1)

Present Simple

1 **T 14** Look at the photographs. Read and listen to the texts.

Sister Mary comes from Ireland. She is a nun and she lives and works in a girls' school in Cork. She teaches French and Spanish. She likes her job and she loves the green countryside of Ireland. She goes walking in her free time.

Hans Huser is a ski-instructor. He is Swiss and lives in Villars, a village in the mountains. In summer he works in a sports shop and in winter he teaches skiing. He speaks four languages, French, German, Italian, and English. He is married and has two sons. He plays football with them in his free time.

● Grammar questions

– Underline the verbs in the texts.

  Examples
  comes   is

– What is the last letter of these verbs?

2 In pairs, practise saying the verbs. Read one of the texts aloud.

Practice

1 Grammar

Complete the sentences about Sister Mary and Hans.

a She comes from Ireland. He _____ _____ Switzerland.

b He lives in a village, but she _____ _____ a town.

c She works in a school. He _____ _____ a sports shop.

d He _____ skiing. She _____ _____ and Spanish.

e She _____ near the sea, but he _____ in the mountains.

f He likes his job and she _____ _____ _____ , too.

g He _____ _____ sons.

h She _____ walking in her free time. He _____ _____ with his sons.

i He _____ four languages. She _____ three.

19

2 Speaking

Look at the photograph of Georges and the information.
Make sentences about him.

> Georges is a taxi driver. He comes from France and he lives in Paris.

> He works ...

> He isn't ...

> He has ...

> ... in his free time.

In pairs, talk about Keiko and Mark.

Georges Teste	a taxi driver
Country	France
Town	Paris
Place of work	in the centre of Paris
Married?	No
Family	a dog (!)
Free time	walking with his dog and football

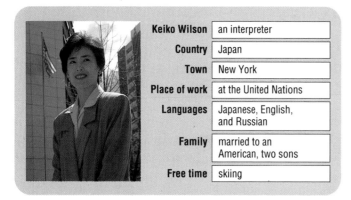

Keiko Wilson	an interpreter
Country	Japan
Town	New York
Place of work	at the United Nations
Languages	Japanese, English, and Russian
Family	married to an American, two sons
Free time	skiing

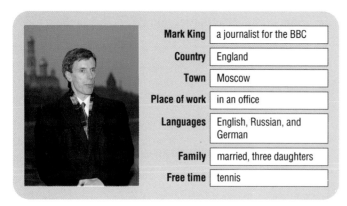

Mark King	a journalist for the BBC
Country	England
Town	Moscow
Place of work	in an office
Languages	English, Russian, and German
Family	married, three daughters
Free time	tennis

3 Writing

Write about a friend, or your mother or father.

Example

My friend Anna is a student. She lives in ...

20

PRESENTATION (2)

Questions and negatives

1 **T 15a** Read and listen to the questions and answers.
Practise saying them.

Where does Sister Mary come from?	Ireland.
What does she do?	She's a teacher.
Does she speak French?	Yes, she does.
Does she speak German?	No, she doesn't.

> 1 *Does* is an auxiliary verb in questions with *he*, *she*, and *it*.
> *Doesn't* (= *does not*) is in negative sentences.
>
> She come **s** from Ireland.
>
> Where **does** she come from? She **does** n't come from England.
>
> 2 Notice the pronunciation of *does* and *doesn't*.
> /dəz/   /dʌz/   /dʌznt/
> Does she speak French? Yes, she does./No, she doesn't.
>
> 3 Where does she come from? = Where's she from?
>
> 4 What does he do? = What's his job?

2 Complete the questions and answers.

a Where _____ Hans _____ from? Switzerland.

b What _____ he _____ ? He's a ski-instructor.

c _____ he _____ French and German? Yes, he _____ .

d _____ he _____ Spanish? No, he _____ .

T 15b Listen and check.

Practice

1 Writing and speaking

1 Write questions about Georges, Keiko, and Mark.

Example

Where/come from? *Where does he come from?*

a Where/live?
b What/do?
c Where/work?
d Does he/she speak French/Spanish ...?
e What ... in his/her free time?
f ... play tennis?
g How many children ...?
h ... a dog?

2 Work in pairs. Ask and answer your questions, but don't look at the information.

3 Now ask your partner the same questions about a member of his or her family.

2 Listening and pronunciation

1 **T 16a** Listen to the sentences about Georges, Keiko, and Mark. Some are right and some are wrong. Correct the wrong sentences.

Example

Georges comes from Paris. (Yes, that's right.)

Georges lives in London. (No, he doesn't. He lives in Paris.)

2 **T 16b** Tick (✔) the sentence you hear.

1 a He likes his job.
  b She likes her job.
2 a She loves walking.
  b She loves working.
3 a She's married.
  b She isn't married.
4 a Does she have three children?
  b Does he have three children?
5 a What does he do?
  b Where does he go?
6 a She watches the television.
  b She washes the television.

3 Choosing the correct sentence

One sentence has a mistake. Choose the correct sentence. Put ✔ and ✗.

1 a She comes from Spain.
  b She come from Spain.
2 a What he do in his free time?
  b What does he do in his free time?
3 a Where lives she?
  b Where does she live?
4 a He isn't married.
  b He doesn't married.
5 a Does she has two sons?
  b Does she have two sons?
6 a He doesn't play football.
  b He no plays football.
7 a She doesn't love Peter.
  b She doesn't loves Peter.
8 a What's he's address?
  b What's his address?

● VOCABULARY AND PRONUNCIATION

Jobs

1 Use your dictionary and match a picture with a job in column A.

2 Match a line in A with a line in B.

A	B
f A pilot	makes bread.
___ An interpreter	looks after people in hospital.
___ A hairdresser	writes for a newspaper.
___ A singer	works in a hotel.
___ A nurse	translates things.
___ An actor	sells things.
___ A mechanic	flies a plane.
___ A journalist	works in a night club.
___ A receptionist	cuts hair.
___ A baker	mends cars.
___ A shop assistant	makes films.

3 Look at the phonetic spelling of some of the words. Practise saying them.

a /nɜːs/   b /ɪntɜːprɪtə/   c /rɪsepʃənɪst/
d /æktə/   e /sɪŋə/   f /məkænɪk/

4 Memorize the lines in A and B! Close your books. Ask and answer questions.

21

READING AND LISTENING

Pre-reading task

1 Look at the map. Which two countries are they?
Write the names of the capital cities on the map.

2 Check the meaning of the <u>underlined</u> words in your dictionary.
He <u>leaves</u> home.
She <u>drives</u> to work.
He <u>catches</u> a train at 9.00.
a <u>ferry</u>
She <u>arrives</u> at work at 8.30.
The <u>journey</u> <u>takes</u> twenty minutes.
It <u>costs</u> <u>only</u> ten pence.
<u>fortunately</u>

Reading

Read the text. Answer the three questions.

a Where does Mr Garret live?
b What's his job?
c Where does he work?

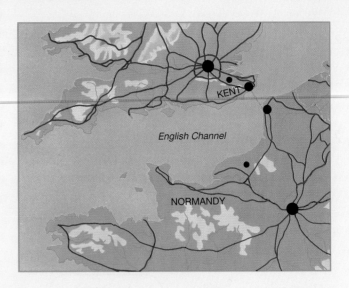

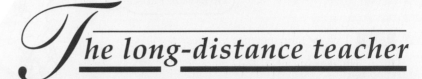

The long-distance teacher

Mr Frank Garret, 65, is a schoolteacher. He is English, but he lives in France, in the Normandy village of Yerville. Mr Garret lives in France, but he works in England.

Every Monday he leaves home at 2.30 in the morning and drives 101 miles from his village to Boulogne, where he leaves his car and catches the ferry to Folkestone. Then he catches the train to Maidstone in Kent and he arrives at Manor School at 8.25. He teaches French from 9.00 in the morning to 3.30 in the afternoon, and then leaves school. He arrives home at 9.30 in the evening. The journey there and back takes twelve hours and costs only £16!

Fortunately, Mr Garret works in England only one day a week.

And what does he do on the other days? He teaches English! He has a class of eighteen French students in Yerville.

'Yes, on Tuesdays I'm tired,' he says, 'but I love my job in England and I love my home in France. I'm a happy man!'

Comprehension check

1 Write Folkestone, Boulogne, Maidstone, and Yerville on the map. Mark Mr Garret's journey.

2 Answer the questions.

  a Is Mr Garret French?
  b How many jobs does he have?
  c Does he go to Boulogne by train?
  d Where does he leave his car?
  e Where does he catch the train?
  f Is the journey cheap or expensive? How much does it cost?
  g Does Mr Garret go to Manor School every day?
  h Why does Mr Garret live in France but work in England? (*Because ...*)

3 Complete the text about Mr Garret's journey back home from his school.

Mr Garret _____ Manor School at 3.30 in the afternoon

and he _____ the train to Folkestone, where he _____

the ferry to Boulogne.

Then he _____ from Boulogne back to his village. The

journey _____ six hours. He _____ home at 9.30.

Language work

Complete the questions.

Example
What time *does he leave* home in the morning?
At 2.30.

  a What time _____ _____ _____ at Manor School?
    At 8.25.
  b What time _____ _____ _____ ?
    At 3.30.
  c When _____ _____ _____ home in the evening?
    At 9.30.
  d How much _____ the journey _____ ?
    Sixteen pounds.
  e How long _____ the journey home _____ ?
    Six hours.
  f How many students _____ he _____ in his English class?
    Eighteen.

Listening and speaking

1 **T 17** Listen to five conversations from Frank Garret's day and complete them.

  a A _____ _____ , sir. Can I see your _____ ?
    B Yes, of course. Here you _____ .
    A Thank you. Maidstone next _____ .
    B Thank you.

  b A _____ _____ , boys and girls.
    B _____ _____ , Mr Garret.
    A _____ _____ _____ your homework, please?
    B It's on your _____ , Mr Garret.
    A Thank you.

  c A _____ , Frank. Have a good _____ .
    B Thank you very _____ .
    A See you next _____ !
    B Yes, _____ course. Goodbye!

  d A _____ _____ . Is this seat _____ ?
    B Yes, it is.
    A Thank you. It's _____ this evening.
    B _____ certainly _____ . And the sea's very _____ !

  e A Hello, darling! Are you _____ ?
    B Yes, I am. And _____ .
    A Sit down and _____ a glass of wine.
    B Mmmm! Thank you. I'm _____ , too.

2 What time of day is it, morning, afternoon, or evening? Where are they? Who are the people? Choose from the boxes.

Places	People
at home	Frank's wife
on the ferry	a teacher
on the train	school children
at school	a ticket inspector
	a ferry passenger

3 Work in pairs and practise the conversations.

● EVERYDAY ENGLISH

What time is it?

1 Look at the clocks. Write the times. Practise saying them.

It's five o'clock. _____

It's half past five. _____

It's quarter past five. _____

It's quarter to six. _____

It's five past five. _____

It's twenty-five past five.

_____ It's twenty to six.

It's ten to six. _____

T 18a Listen and check.

2 Look at the times.

It's exactly half past three.

It's nearly half past three.

It's just after half past three.

3 **T 18b** In pairs, draw clocks on a piece of paper. Practise the conversations.

> Excuse me. Can you tell me the time, please?

> Yes, of course. It's six o'clock.

> Thanks.

> I'm sorry. I don't know. I don't have a watch.

24

GRAMMAR SUMMARY

Present Simple *he, she, it*

Positive

He She It	lives	in the mountains.

Have is irregular.
She **has** a dog.   NOT ~~she haves~~

Negative

He She It	does not	live	in France.

doesn't = does not

Question

Where	does	he she it	live?

Yes/No questions   **Short answers**

Does	he she it	live	in France? in the mountains?

Yes, he does.
No, she doesn't.
Yes, it does.

Prepositions

She works **in** a girls' school.
He lives **in** a village **in** the mountains.
In winter he teaches skiing.

On Tuesdays I'm tired.

He plays football **with** his sons **in** his free time.
She is married **to** an American.
A nurse looks **after** people in a hospital.

He arrives **at** school **at** 8.45.
He catches a train **to** London.
He drives **from** his village **to** Boulogne.
He goes **to** Boulogne **by** train.

No preposition

He leaves ___ home at 8.00.
He arrives ___ home at 9.30.

Study the Word List for this unit on page 123.

Present Simple (2) – Articles – Social English

Free time

PRESENTATION (1)

Present Simple

1   Practise saying the days of the week round the class.

2   Look at the photograph and read about Ann McGregor.

Ann McGregor lives in London. She is thirty-four and works for the BBC. She interviews people on an early morning news programme called The World Today. Every weekday she gets up at 3.00 in the morning because the programme starts at 6.30. She loves her work because it is exciting and she meets a lot of very interesting people, but she loves her weekends, too.

3   Look at the verbs in the box. Check the meaning of new verbs in your dictionary.

love	relax	stay	cook	have	like
chat	eat	go	live	arrive	come
visit	bring	listen	go out	get up	leave

4   **T 19a**   Read and listen to what Ann says about her weekends.

On Fridays I _____ home from the BBC at about 2.00 in the afternoon and I just _____ .

On Friday evenings I don't _____ , but sometimes a friend _____ for dinner. He or she _____ the wine and I _____ the meal. I _____ cooking! We _____ to music or we just _____ .

On Saturday mornings I _____ at 9.00 and I _____ shopping. Then in the evenings I sometimes _____ to the theatre or the opera with a friend. I _____ opera! Then we _____ in my favourite Chinese restaurant.

On Sunday... Oh, on Sunday mornings I _____ in bed late, I don't _____ until 11.00! Sometimes in the afternoon I _____ my sister. She _____ in the country and _____ two children. I _____ playing with my niece and nephew, but I _____ early because I _____ to bed at 8.00 on Sunday evenings!

5   Fill in the gaps with the correct form of the verbs in the box. Listen again and check. Read the text aloud.

● Grammar questions

–   Find four verbs which end in -s. Why do they end in -s?

–   Find two negatives.

–   Complete the rules.
   In the Present Simple positive we add _____ to the verb with *he*, *she*, and *it*, but not with *I*, *you*, *we*, and *they*.
   With *I*, *you*, *we*, and *they*, the negative is _____ + infinitive. With *he*, *she*, and *it*, the negative is _____ + infinitive.

25

PRESENTATION (2)

Questions

1 **T 19b** Read and listen to the questions and answers. Practise saying them.

Do you go out on Friday afternoons?   No, I don't.

What do you do?   I just relax.

Do you stay at home on Friday evenings?   Yes, I do.

What do you do?   I cook dinner for friends.

2 Work in pairs. One of you is Ann McGregor. Ask and answer questions about:

Saturday mornings/evenings

Sunday mornings/afternoons/evenings

● Grammar question

Complete the rule.

The auxiliary verb in questions with *I, you, we,* and *they* is

_____ . With *he, she,* and *it* the auxiliary verb is _____ .

Practice

1 Questions and answers

Match a line in A with a line in B to make a question. Then find an answer in C.

Questions		Answers
A	B	C
What time	do you like your job?	My grandmother.
Where	do you travel to work?	To a disco.
What	do you go on Saturday evenings?	After dinner.
When	do you visit on Sundays?	At 11 o'clock.
Who	do you go to bed?	I watch TV.
Why	do you do in the evenings?	Because it's interesting.
How	do you do your homework?	By train.

2 Speaking

1 Work in pairs. Ask and answer questions about your weekdays and weekends.

What time do you get up on weekdays?   At 7.00.

Do you go out on Friday evenings?   Yes, I do.

Where do you go?   To the disco.

2 Tell the class about you and your partner.

Maria goes to the disco on Friday evenings and I usually watch TV.

3 Listening and pronunciation

T 20 Tick (✔) the sentence you hear.

1 a What does he do on Sundays?
   b What does she do on Sundays?

2 a I stay at home on Tuesday evenings.
   b I stay at home on Thursday evenings.

3 a He lives here.
   b He leaves here.

4 a I read a lot.
   b I eat a lot.

5 a Where do you go on Saturday evenings?
   b What do you do on Saturday evenings?

6 a She likes cars.
   b She likes cards.

4 Speaking and writing

1 Look at the questionnaire. Ask your teacher the questions, then ask two other students. Put ✔ or ✗ in the columns.

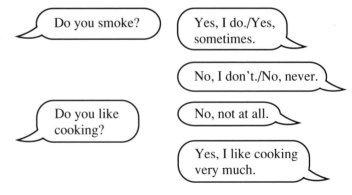

Do you smoke?   Yes, I do./Yes, sometimes.

No, I don't./No, never.

Do you like cooking?   No, not at all.

Yes, I like cooking very much.

2 Now answer the questions about you.

Questions	T	S 1	S 2	Me
smoke?	☐	☐	☐	☐
drink wine?	☐	☐	☐	☐
like Chinese food?	☐	☐	☐	☐
like cooking?	☐	☐	☐	☐
play cards?	☐	☐	☐	☐
play tennis?	☐	☐	☐	☐
read a lot?	☐	☐	☐	☐
listen to music a lot?	☐	☐	☐	☐
watch TV a lot?	☐	☐	☐	☐

3   Use the information in the questionnaire. Write about
    you and your teacher, or you and another student.

    Example
    *I don't smoke, but Marc smokes a lot. We both like
    Chinese food. ...*

5 Grammar

Make the positive sentences negative and make the negative
sentences positive.

Examples
She's French.   *She isn't French.*
I don't like cooking.   *I like cooking.*

   a   She doesn't speak German.
   b   They want to learn English.
   c   We're tired and we want to go to bed.
   d   John likes watching football on TV, but he doesn't like
       playing it.
   e   I work at home because I have a word processor.
   f   Sarah isn't happy because she doesn't have a nice flat.
   g   I smoke, I drink, and I don't go to bed early.
   h   He doesn't smoke, he doesn't drink, and he goes to bed
       early.

PRESENTATION (3)

Articles

1   Read the text about the Forrester family. Put *a*, *the*, or
    nothing into the gaps.

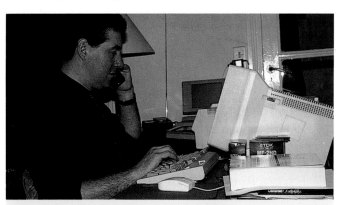

Mr and Mrs Forrester have (a) _____ son and (b) _____
daughter. (c) _____ son lives at (d) _____ home and (e) _____
daughter is (f) _____ student at (g) _____ university. Mr
Forrester is (h) _____ journalist. He works for (i) _____ *Times*.
He writes (j) _____ articles about (k) _____ restaurants. 'I love
(l) _____ food!' he says.

T 21a   Listen and check.

2   Read about articles in the Grammar Summary on page 31.

3   Mr Forrester talks about his holidays. Put *a*, *the*, or
    nothing into the gaps.

'Every spring (a) _____
children go skiing, so my wife
and I go to Paris on
(b) _____ holiday. We stay in
(c) _____ hotel near
(d) _____ River Seine. We
have (e) _____ breakfast in
(f) _____ hotel, but we have
(g) _____ lunch in a
restaurant. (h) _____ French
food is delicious! We walk a
lot, but sometimes we go by
(i) _____ taxi. After four days
we don't want to go (j) _____
home and go back to
(k) _____ work.'

T 21b   Listen and check.

Practice

1 Listening and speaking

Listen to your teacher say some incorrect sentences about the Forresters. Correct the sentences.

Example

The son lives with friends.

> No, he doesn't. He lives at home with his parents.

2 Grammar

Put *a*, *the*, or nothing into the gaps.

a Oxford is _____ town in _____ England, on _____ River Thames.

b _____ Queen lives in _____ very big house in London.

c I have _____ breakfast in _____ bed on _____ Sundays.

d Do you go to _____ work by _____ car?

e My sister is _____ student. She comes _____ home at weekends.

f Do you like _____ Chinese food?

3 Choosing the correct sentence

One sentence has a mistake. Choose the correct sentence. Put ✔ and ✗.

1 a Where do they live?
   b Where they live?
2 a She goes to home by taxi.
   b She goes home by taxi.
3 a Mr and Mrs Smith go walking in summer.
   b Mr and Mrs Smith goes walking in summer.
4 a I don't understand the question.
   b I no understand the question.
5 a She goes at weekends swimming.
   b She goes swimming at weekends.
6 a What you do on Sunday mornings?
   b What do you do on Sunday mornings?
7 a Do you play tennis sometimes?
   b You play tennis sometimes?
8 a I like very much football.
   b I like football very much.
9 a He doesn't know the answer.
   b He don't know the answer.

● VOCABULARY

Free time activities

1 Check the meaning of new words in your dictionary. Match a picture with an activity.

dancing
visiting museums
doing crosswords
walking
skiing
listening to music
watching TV
taking photographs
ice-skating
cooking
playing computer games
sailing
painting
swimming
reading
eating in restaurants
going to the cinema
playing volleyball
windsurfing
sunbathing
playing cards
fishing

2 Work in pairs.
Tell your partner what you like doing and what you don't like doing from the list.
Ask questions about the activities.

> I don't like watching TV, but I like reading very much.

> Oh, really? What do you read?

> When do you read?

Think of two things you like doing which are not on the list. Tell your partner.

● READING AND LISTENING

1 What season is it now? What are the seasons?
What month is it now? What are the months?
When are the different seasons in your country?

2 **T 22a** Read and listen to three people from different
countries talking about their free time.

AL WHEELER FROM CANADA

We have long, cold winters and short, hot summers. In summer I go sailing and I play baseball, but in winter I play ice hockey and go ice-skating. We have a holiday home near a lake, so I go fishing a lot, too. My favourite season is autumn, or fall, as we say in North America. I love the colours of the trees – red, gold, orange, yellow, and brown.

MANUELA DA SILVA FROM PORTUGAL

People think it's always warm and sunny in Portugal, but January and February are often cold, wet, and grey. I don't like winter. I meet friends in restaurants and bars and we chat. Sometimes we go to a Brazilian bar. I love Brazilian music. But then suddenly it's summer and at weekends we drive to the beach, sunbathe, and go windsurfing. I love summer.

TOSHI SUZUKI FROM JAPAN

I work for Pentax cameras, in the export department. I don't have a lot of free time, but I have one special hobby – taking photographs, of course! I like taking photographs of flowers, especially in spring. Sometimes, after work, I relax in a bar near my office with friends. My friend, Shigeru, likes singing pop songs in the bar. This has a special name, Karaoke. I don't sing – I'm too shy! I just watch him.

Comprehension check

1 Answer the questions.
 a Do they all play sports?
 b What do Al and Manuela do in winter?
 c Do Manuela and Toshi like going to bars?
 d Where is Al's holiday home?
 e When does Toshi like taking photographs of flowers?
 f What do Manuela and her friends do in summer?
 g Do you know all their jobs?
 h Why does Al like autumn?
 i Who does Toshi watch? Why doesn't Toshi sing?
 j Which colours are in the texts?

2 Find five mistakes in this summary and correct them.

> Al comes from Canada. In winter he plays ice hockey and goes skiing. He has a holiday home near the sea.
>
> Manuela comes from Brazil. She likes sunbathing and windsurfing in summer.
>
> Toshi comes from Japan. He has a lot of free time. He likes taking photographs and singing pop songs in bars.

3 **T 22b** Listen to the conversations. Is it Al, Manuela, or Toshi? Where are they? How do you know?

4 What is your favourite season? Why? What do you do in the different seasons?

Vocabulary

Write *play* or *go*.

_____ football	_____ walking	_____ sailing
_____ swimming	_____ volleyball	_____ tennis
_____ golf	_____ ice-skating	_____ dancing
_____ ice hockey	_____ windsurfing	_____ skiing
_____ fishing	_____ baseball	

● EVERYDAY ENGLISH

Social English

1 Complete the conversations with the sentences on the right.

c A _____ . It's very hot in here.

B _____ . I'm quite cold.

A OK. _____ .

Really?
Can I open the window?
It doesn't matter.

a A _____ .

B Yes?

A Do you have a light?

B _____ . I don't smoke.

A _____ .

I'm sorry.
Excuse me!
That's OK.

d A _____ .

B Can I help you?

A Can I have a film for my camera?

B How many exposures?

A _____ .

B How many exposures?

A _____ .

B How many pictures? 24? 36?

A Ah! _____ . 36, please.

Pardon?
Now I understand!
Excuse me!
What does 'exposures' mean?

b A _____ . The traffic is bad today.

B _____ . Come and sit down. We're on page 25.

Don't worry.
I'm sorry I'm late.

T 23 Listen and check.

2 In pairs, practise the conversations.

30

GRAMMAR SUMMARY

Present Simple

Positive

I You We They	start	
		at 6.30.
He She It	starts	

Negative

I You We They	don't		
		start	at 6.30.
He She It	doesn't		

Question

When	do	I you we they	start?
	does	he she it	

Yes/No questions

Do	you they	have	a camera?
Does	he she it	like	Chinese food?

Short answers

No, I don't./No, we don't.
Yes, they do.

Yes, he does.
No, she doesn't.
Yes, it does.

like/love + verb + *-ing*

When *like* and *love* are followed by a verb, it is usually verb + *-ing*.

   I like swim**ming**.
   She loves listen**ing** to music.
   They like sail**ing** very much.

Articles

a = **indefinite article**

1   She has **a** flat in London.
    Can I have **a** ham sandwich?
2   She's **a** nurse. (jobs)

the = **definite article**

3   **The** flat (= her flat) is very nice.
    The ham sandwich is horrible!
4   **The** Times; **the** Thames (newspapers and rivers)

No article

5   **Things in general**

    I have ___ tea and toast for breakfast.

    ___ Books are expensive.

    I like taking ___ photographs.

    Do you like ___ Chinese food?

6   **Meals, places, transport**

    I have ___ breakfast/lunch/dinner.

    I go/come ___ home.

    I go/come to ___ school/university/work/bed.

    I'm at ___ work/on ___ holiday.

    I go/come by ___ train/car/bus/taxi.

Prepositions

I stay in bed **until** 11.00.
She works **for** the BBC.
We listen **to** music.

on	Friday mornings/evenings
	Saturday

at weekends

in	the morning/evening
	(the) spring

We stay **in** a hotel.

Study the Word List for this unit on page 123.

STOP AND CHECK

Units 1–4

1 Correcting the mistakes

Each sentence has a mistake. Find it and correct it!

Example
Antonia is ~~Italiana~~.   *Antonia is Italian.*

a   London is a city very big.
b   My mother works in a hotel is a receptionist.
c   My father watch TV in the evening.
d   He's like watching football.
e   On Sundays we go in a restaurant.
f   Hans is businessman.
g   You family is very nice.
h   I like listen to music.
i   Our school have a lot of students.
j   The childrens go to school near here.
k   We have the dinner at 7.00.
l   Buses in London are reds.
m   My brother no have a job.
n   Do you want a ice-cream?
o   Is near here, my flat.

`15`

2 Word order

Put the words in the correct order.

Example
Madrid Jorge from comes   *Jorge comes from Madrid.*

a   policeman   from   is   John   a   New York

_____ .

b   married   sister   is   your?

_____ ?

c   mountains   sister   skiing   goes   the   in   my

_____ .

d   isn't   coffee   nice   English   very

_____ .

e   your   what   name   teacher's   is?

_____ ?

f   surname   how   spell   do   your   you?

_____ ?

g   often   weekends   go   I   at   swimming

_____ .

`7`

3 Choosing the correct sentence

One sentence is correct. Which one?

Example
Where she from?   ✗
Where does she from?   ✗
Where is she from?   ✔

1   a   Sally is a nice girl, and I like.
    b   Sally is a nice girl, and I like her.
    c   Sally is a nice girl, and I like him.
2   a   Coffee English is horrible.
    b   The English coffee is horrible.
    c   English coffee is horrible.
3   a   Peter works with his father.
    b   Peter works with he's father.
    c   Peter works with him father.
4   a   Sally and Tim live in Madrid. They're flat is lovely.
    b   Sally and Tim live in Madrid. Their flat is lovely.
    c   Sally and Tim live in Madrid. There flat is lovely.
5   a   She lives in a house or a flat?
    b   Does she lives in a house or a flat?
    c   Does she live in a house or a flat?
6   a   I don't like going to discos.
    b   I don't like go to discos.
    c   I no like going to discos.
7   a   How many languages you speak?
    b   How many languages do you speak?
    c   How many languages does you speak?
8   a   My brother work in a bank.
    b   My brother he works in a bank.
    c   My brother works in a bank.

`8`

4 Questions

1   Match a line in A with a line in B to make a question.

A	B
What	do you go to bed?
Where	languages do you speak?
What time	is a cup of coffee and a sandwich?
Who	do you usually sit next to?
How much	do you do at weekends?
How many	do you go on holiday?

`5`

32

2 Here are the answers to some questions. Write the questions. Use the words in brackets.

Example
What do you do? (you / do)   I'm a hairdresser.

a _____ ?
(Peter / start work)   At 8.00.

b _____ ?
(Sylvie and Jacques / come)   From France.

c _____ ?
(your wife's)   Jackie.

d _____ ?
(you / have)   Three. Two girls and a boy.

e _____ ?
(you / like / gardening)   Yes, I do. I grow
a lot of vegetables.

[5]

5 Prepositions

Put a preposition from the box into each gap.

| at   in   about   after   for   with   by   to   on   after |

James lives ___in___ a small flat (a) _____ Cambridge. He lives
(b) _____ two other boys who are students (c) _____ Cambridge
University. They work hard during the week, but (d) _____
weekends they invite a lot of friends to their house. They cook a
meal (e) _____ their friends, and then they go out (f) _____ the
pub (g) _____ a drink, or they stay (h) _____ home and listen
(i) _____ music.
James has two jobs. (j) _____ Mondays, Tuesdays, and
Wednesdays he works (k) _____ a hospital, where he helps to
look (l) _____ children who are ill. He goes to the hospital
(m) _____ bus. He starts (n) _____ ten o'clock and works until
quarter (o) _____ five. On Thursdays and Fridays he works
(p) _____ home. He has a word processor (q) _____ his bedroom
and he writes stories. (r) _____ the evening, one of the boys cooks
a meal. (s) _____ dinner they look in the newspaper to see what's
on TV or they talk (t) _____ their day. They usually go to bed at
about midnight.

[20]

6 Vocabulary

Put the words into the correct columns. There are five
words for each column.

| cheese   map   actor   favourite   toast   dentist   arrive
palace   ham   village   want   bring   notebook   easy
expensive   chicken   journalist   dictionary   leave   friendly
interpreter   magazine   orange   night club   beach   engineer
office   newspaper   funny   listen |

Things to read	Professions	Things to eat	Places	Verbs	Adjectives
		cheese			

[30]

7 *am/is/do/does (not)*

Put a verb from the box into each gap.

| am/'m not   is/isn't   are/aren't   does/doesn't   do/don't |

Example
I *'m not* English, I'm French.

a Vienna _____ in Austria.
b Where _____ you from?
c I _____ on holiday. I'm at work.
d My teacher _____ very funny.
e What time _____ the bank open?
f My sister _____ eat meat because she _____ like it.
g I _____ hungry. How much _____ a cheese
   sandwich?
h Where _____ you usually go on holiday?
i Daddy, we _____ want to go to bed. We _____ tired.
j Learning English _____ boring!
   It's interesting!

[10]

Total [100]

TRANSLATE

Translate the sentences into your language. Translate the
ideas, not word by word.

1 I am a student.
_____

2 My sister isn't at home. She's at work.
_____

3 I live in a flat.
_____

4 My mother works in a bank.
_____

5 I don't smoke.
_____

6 My father doesn't like rock music.
_____

7 What do you do at weekends?
_____

8 John's flat is in the centre of town.
_____

9 Can I have a cup of coffee, please?
_____

33

UNIT 5

There is/are – Prepositions – any/some – Directions (1)

Places

PRESENTATION (1)

There is/are – any – Prepositions

1   What are the names of the rooms in a house? Think of one or two things that we do in the rooms.

> We watch TV in the living room.

2   Look at the photograph of a living room.
    Find these objects.

a chair	an armchair	a table	a sofa	a window
a picture	a telephone	a television	a lamp	
a mirror	a stereo	a fire	a plant	

3   Describe the room.

> There's a sofa.   There's a television.

> There are two lamps and an armchair.

4   **T 24** Listen to the questions and answers, and practise saying them.

Is there a stereo?	Yes, there is.
Is there a clock?	No, there isn't.
Are there any books?	Yes, there are.
Are there any magazines?	No, there aren't.

In pairs, ask and answer questions about these objects.

a table	a dog	a desk	lamps	pictures
a fire	a stereo	a camera	flowers	plants
a mirror	an armchair	a newspaper	photos	books

5 Look at the photograph of the living room. Put a
   preposition from the box into each gap.

near	on	next to	in front of	behind

   a The telephone is _____ the table.
   b The table is _____ the sofa.
   c The chair is _____ the stereo.
   d The lamp is _____ the chair.
   e The dog is _____ the fire.

Practice

1 Grammar

Complete the sentences about the living room in the
photograph.

   a There _____ two books _____ the sofa.
   b The sofa is _____ _____ _____ the window.
   c There _____ a lamp _____ _____ the television.
   d The telephone is _____ one of the lamps.
   e '_____ there _____ pictures on the wall?'
      'Yes, _____ _____ .'
   f There _____ _____ desk.
   g There's a plant _____ the sofa in front of the window.
   h Is _____ _____ fire?
   i '_____ there _____ people in the living room?'
      'No, _____ _____ .'

2 Speaking and listening

1 Work in pairs.
   Your teacher will give you each a picture of a living
   room. There are ten differences! Don't show your
   picture!
   Talk about the pictures to find the ten differences.

   (Is there a table?)   (Yes, there is.)
   (How many people   (Two, and there's a
     are there?)   cat on the sofa.)

2 **T 25** Look at the pictures together. Listen to someone
   describing them. There are five mistakes in each
   description. Say 'Stop!' when you hear a mistake.

   (Stop! There aren't three people! There are four people!)

PRESENTATION (2)

some and *any*

1 Look at the photograph of the kitchen. What can you see?

2 **T 26** Listen to the description of the kitchen and fill in
   the gaps.

It's a modern kitchen, nice and clean with a lot of cupboards.
_____'s a washing machine, a fridge, and a cooker, but there
isn't a dishwasher. There are some lovely _____ on the walls,
but there aren't any photographs. There's a radio _____ the
cooker. There are some flowers, but there aren't _____
plants. On the table there are some apples and oranges. Ah!
And there are _____ cups and plates next to the sink.

● Grammar questions

– Look at the sentences. When do we say *There isn't a ...* and when do we say *There aren't any ...?*

> There isn't a dishwasher.
> There aren't any photographs.

– Look at the sentences. What is the difference?

> There are two books.
> There are some flowers.

> 1   When we use *some*, we are not interested in the exact number.
>
>> I have ten fingers. (NOT I have ~~some~~ fingers.)
>> I have some friends in Berlin.
>
> 2   We use *any* in questions and negatives.
>
>> Are there any photographs?
>> There aren't any people.
>
> 3   Notice the pronunciation of *some* and *any*.
>
>> /səm/   /enɪ/
>> There are some flowers. There aren't any plants.

Practice

1 Speaking

1   Look again at the photograph of the kitchen. Make sentences with *There's a ...* and *There are some ...* about the kitchen.

> There's a fridge.   There are some flowers.

2   Have a class discussion.
What is there in *your* kitchen? How is your kitchen different from the one in the picture?
Why do you think kitchens are different in different parts of the world?

2 Grammar

1   Put *some* or *any* into the gaps.

a   In our classroom there are _____ books on the floor.

b   There aren't _____ flowers.

c   Are there _____ German students in your class?

d   There aren't _____ Chinese students.

e   We have _____ dictionaries in the cupboard.

f   There are _____ pens on the table.

2   What is there in your classroom?

3 Listening and speaking

1   **T 27**   Listen to a man describing what is in his briefcase. Tick (✔) the things you hear.

___ a newspaper   ___ some pens   ___ a bus ticket
___ a dictionary   ___ a notebook   ___ an address book
___ a sandwich   ___ a letter   ___ some stamps
___ some keys   ___ some photos

2   What is there in *your* bag?

4 Choosing the correct sentence

One sentence has a mistake. Choose the correct sentence. Put ✔ and ✗.

1   a   There's a dog in front of the fire.
    b   There's in front of the fire a dog.
2   a   There isn't a desk in the room.
    b   There isn't an desk in the room.
3   a   Near of my house there's a park.
    b   Near my house there's a park.
4   a   We eat in the kitchen.
    b   We eat in kitchen.
5   a   We have a fridge, a table, and a cooker.
    b   We have a fridge, a table, and any cooker.
6   a   My room isn't big, but I like it very much.
    b   My room isn't big, but I like very much.
7   a   There isn't television in the living room.
    b   There isn't a television in the living room.
8   a   In the evening my mother go for a walk.
    b   In the evening my mother goes for a walk.
9   a   He gets up at 7.00 every day.
    b   He's get up at 7.00 every day.

● READING

Pre-reading task

1   Look at the photographs. Can you answer these questions?

Where are these buildings?
What are they?
Who lives in them?

2　Check the meaning of new words in your dictionary or with your teacher.

inside (*prep*)	to prepare (*v*)	do the washing-up (*v*)
the whole world	own (*adj*)	everybody (*pron*)
famous (*adj*)	piper (*n*)	during (*prep*)
grow up (*v*)	outside (*prep*)	course (food) (*n*)
like (*prep*)		

Reading

Read the text.

INSIDE

Buckingham Palace

THE PALACE

There are two addresses in London that the whole world knows. One is 10 Downing Street, where the Prime Minister lives. The other is Buckingham Palace. This famous palace, first built in 1703, is in the very centre of London.

It is two places, not one. It is a family house, where children play and grow up. It is also the place where presidents, kings, and politicians go to meet the Queen.

Buckingham Palace is like a small town, with a police station, two post offices, a hospital, a bar, two sports clubs, a disco, a cinema, and a swimming pool. There are 600 rooms and three miles of red carpet. Two men work full-time to look after the 300 clocks. About 700 people work in the Palace.

Comprehension check

1　Are the sentences true (✔) or false (✗)? Correct the false sentences.

   a　The Palace is more than two hundred years old.
   b　It is famous because it is in the centre of London.
   c　The same person starts the Queen's bath, prepares her clothes, and feeds the dogs.
   d　The dogs sleep in the Queen's bedroom.
   e　The Queen and the Prime Minister go out for a drink on Tuesday nights.

2　Answer the questions.

   a　'Buckingham Palace is two places, not one.' How?
   b　Why is it like a small town?
   c　Are there a lot of clocks?
   d　How many dogs does the Queen have?
   e　What newspaper does she read?
   f　What sort of music does the piper play?
   g　Why do people have five glasses on the table?
   h　Who does the Queen speak to during a meal?
   i　What happens when the Queen finishes her food?

THE QUEEN'S DAY

When the Queen gets up in the morning, seven people look after her. One starts her bath, one prepares her clothes, and one feeds the Royal dogs. She has eight or nine dogs, and they sleep in their own bedroom near the Queen's bedroom. Two people bring her breakfast. She has coffee from Harrods, toast, and eggs. Every day for fifteen minutes, a piper plays Scottish music outside her room and the Queen reads *The Times*.

Every Tuesday evening, she meets the Prime Minister. They talk about world news and have a drink, perhaps a gin and tonic or a whisky.

AN INVITATION TO THE PALACE

When the Queen invites a lot of people for dinner, it takes three days to prepare the table and three days to do the washing-up. Everybody has five glasses: one for red wine, one for white

wine, one for water, one for port, and one for liqueur. During the first and second courses, the Queen speaks to the person on her left and then she speaks to the person on her right for the rest of the meal. When the Queen finishes her food, everybody finishes, and it is time for the next course!

Language work

1 Work in pairs. Ask and answer questions about Buckingham Palace.

> Is there a police station?   Yes, there is.

> Is there a post office?   Yes, there are two.

Ask about:

a swimming pool   a school   a sports club   a disco
a supermarket   a bar   a cinema   a hospital

2 Here are the answers to some questions about the text. Write the questions.

a 10 Downing Street.	d Coffee, toast, and eggs.
b 600.	e In their own bedroom.
c 300.	f On Tuesday evenings.

● VOCABULARY AND PRONUNCIATION

Places, people, food and drink

1 Put words from the text *Inside Buckingham Palace* into the correct columns. Mark the stress on words with two syllables or more.

Places	People	Food and drink
• *palace* *house*	• *Prime Minister* • *family*	• *breakfast* • *coffee*

2 Can you add more words to the columns?

● LISTENING AND SPEAKING

1 **T 28** Listen to five people talking about where they live. Fill in the chart.

	Anne-Marie	Harry	Dave and Maggie	Thanos
House or flat?				
Old or new?				
Where?				
Number of bedrooms?				
Garden?				
Live(s) with?				

2 Talk about where you live.
Do you live in a house or a flat?
How many rooms are there?
Do you have a garden? A terrace?
What's in your bedroom?

Writing

3 Write a paragraph about where you live.

● EVERYDAY ENGLISH

Directions (1)

1 Look at the street map. Where can you buy these things?

bread   a CD   cigarettes   a book   a plane ticket

Where can you borrow a book?

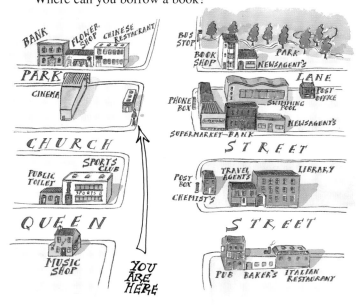

2 **T 29** Listen to the conversations and complete them.

a A Excuse me! Is _____ a chemist's _____ here?
   B Yes. It's over _____ .
   A Thanks.

b A _____ me! Is there a _____ club near here?
   B Yes. _____ _____ Queen Street. Take the
      second _____ _____ _____ right.
   A Thanks.

c A Excuse me! Is there a _____ near here?
   B There's _____ in Church Street _____ _____
      the bank, and there's one in Park Lane opposite
      the _____ _____ .
   A Is that one _____ ?
   B No. Just two minutes, that's all.

d A Is there a cinema near here?
   B _____ the first left, and it's _____ _____ left,
      _____ the flower shop.
   A Thanks a lot.

3 Work in pairs. Practise the conversations. Then make
   more conversations about other places on the map.

4 Talk about where *you* are.
   Is there a chemist's near here? Is it far?
   What about a bank/a post office/a sports club?

GRAMMAR SUMMARY

There is/are

Positive

There	is	a sofa.	(singular)
	are	two books.	(plural)

Negative

There	isn't	an	armchair.	(singular)
	aren't	any	flowers.	(plural)

Yes/No questions **Short answers**

Is	there	a table?
Are		any photos?

Yes, there is.
No, there isn't.
Yes, there are.
No, there aren't.

some/any

Positive
There are some flowers.   *some* + plural noun

Negative
There aren't any cups.   *any* + plural noun

Question
Are there any books?   *any* + plural noun

Prepositions

There is a photo **on** the television.

The bank is **next to** the supermarket.

The bus stop is **near** the park.

There is a post box **in front of** the chemist's.

The cinema is **on** the left, **opposite** the
flower shop.

There are two pictures **on** the wall.

The lamp is **behind** the sofa.

Your dictionary is **like** my dictionary.
She speaks **to** people **during** the meal.
Why don't we go out **for** a drink?
They talk **about** the news.
She has coffee **from** Harrods.

Study the Word List for this unit on page 124.

UNIT 6

can/could – was/were – At the airport

What can you do?

PRESENTATION (1)

can/can't

1 **T 30a** Look at the pictures. Match a sentence with a picture. Then, listen and check.

1 Cats can see in the dark.
2 She can type fifty words a minute.
3 'Can you use a word processor?' 'Yes, I can.'
4 'Can you speak Japanese?' ' No, I can't.'
5 I can't spell your name.
6 I can't hear you. The line's bad.

2 Listen again carefully.

What is the pronunciation of *can*
– in the positive and in questions?
– in short answers?
What is the pronunciation of *can't*?

⚠			
1	I can speak French. Can you speak French?	=	/kən/ or /kn/
	Yes, I can.	=	/kæn/
	I can't speak German.	=	/kɑːnt/
2	Look at the sentence stress.		
	● ● ⬤ I can swim.		● ● ● I can't cook.
3	I can't speak Japanese. NOT I ~~don't can~~ speak Japanese.		

3 **T 30b** Listen and complete the sentences with *can* or *can't* + verb.

a I _____ _____ , but I _____ _____ .

b He _____ _____ and he _____ _____ .

c '_____ you _____ ?' 'Yes, I _____ .'

d They _____ _____ , but they _____ _____ .

e We _____ _____ and we _____ _____ .

f '_____ she _____ ?' 'No, she _____ .'

40

Practice

1 Listening and speaking

1 **T 31** Listen to Sarah. What can she do? What can't she do? Put ✔ or ✘.

drive a car   speak Italian   play the piano   use a word processor

draw   speak German

cook   type

speak Spanish   ski   play tennis   swim   speak French

2 Work in pairs.
Use the words in Exercise 1. Ask and answer questions.

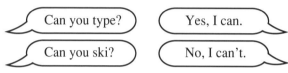

Can you type?   Yes, I can.

Can you ski?   No, I can't.

Tell the class about your partner.

2 Speaking

1 Work in pairs.
Look at the list. Talk about computers.
What can they do? What can't they do?

They can count, but they can't translate.   Yes, they can!

Computers

Can they...?

count	smell
translate	forecast the weather
speak English	check spellings
play chess	make music
do crosswords	have conversations
hear	write books
see	think

---

2 What can people do that computers can't do?

PRESENTATION (2)

was/were – could

1 Read the questions. Check the meaning of new words. Complete the answers.

Present	Past
a What day is it today? It's _____ .	What day was it yesterday? It was _____ .
b What month is it now? It's _____ .	What month was it last month? It was _____ .
c Where are you now? I'm in/at _____ .	Where were you yesterday morning? I was in/at _____ .
d Are you in England? _____ , I am./ _____ , I'm not.	Were you in England in 1990? _____ , I was./ _____ , I wasn't.
e Can you swim? _____ , I can./ _____ , I can't.	Could you swim when you were five? _____ , I could./ _____ , I couldn't.
f Can your teacher cook? Yes, _____ can./No, _____ can't.	Could he/she cook when he/she was sixteen? Yes, _____ could./No, _____ couldn't.

● Grammar questions

– What are the past tense forms of the verb *to be*?

	Positive	Negative
I	*was*	*wasn't*
you	*were*	*weren't*
he/she/it	_____	_____
we	_____	_____
they	_____	_____

– What is the past tense form of *can* in all persons?

Positive   _____   Negative   _____

2 **T 32** Listen and repeat.

3 Ask and answer questions.

Where were you ...
at eight o'clock this morning?   at half past six yesterday evening?

at two o'clock this morning?   at this time yesterday?

at ten o'clock last night?   last Sunday lunchtime?

Practice

1 Listening and pronunciation

1 Read the conversation between two friends, Sue and Bill. Put *was*, *were*, *wasn't*, or *couldn't* into the gaps.

Sue _____ you at Eve's party last Saturday?

Bill Yes, I _____ .

Sue _____ it good?

Bill Well, it _____ OK.

Sue _____ there many people?

Bill Yes, there _____ .

Sue _____ Tom there?

Bill No, he _____ . And where _____ you?

Sue Oh ... I _____ go because I _____ at Adam's party! It _____ brilliant!

T 33 Listen and check. Listen again for the pronunciation of *was* and *were*.

2 Work in pairs. Practise the conversation. Then make similar conversations about:
   John's barbecue last Sunday
   the disco last Friday evening
   the football match last week

2 Speaking

1 Look at the sentences.
      My sister *could* read *when she was* four.
      I *couldn't* read *until I was* seven.
   Make similar sentences, using these words.

   a Mozart/play the piano/three. I/play the piano/ten.
   b Picasso/draw/one. I/draw/six.
   c Nureyev/dance/three. I/dance/seven.
   d I/speak/two. Einstein/speak/eight. (True!)

Memorize some of the sentences! Practise saying them.

2 Match a line in A with a line in B.

A	B
Mozart was born in	Siberia.
Picasso was born in	Ulm.
Nureyev was born in	Salzburg.
Einstein was born in	Malaga.

Where were you born? When?

I was born in Madrid in 1975.

3 Choosing the correct sentence

One sentence has a mistake. Which is the correct sentence? Put ✔ and ✗.

1 a I don't can use a word processor.
   b I can't use a word processor.
2 a Was they at the party?
   b Were they at the party?
3 a I'm sorry. I can't go to the party.
   b I'm sorry. I no can go to the party.
4 a She no was at home.
   b She wasn't at home.
5 a He could play chess when he was five.
   b He can play chess when he was five.
6 a I was in New York the last week.
   b I was in New York last week.

● READING AND SPEAKING

Pre-reading task

What do teenagers like doing in your country?
Think of three things and tell the others in the class.

Reading

Divide into two groups.

Group A   Read about Ivan Mirsky.
Group B   Read about Jaya Rajah.

Answer the questions.

Comprehension check

a   How old is he?
b   Does he go to school?
c   Where was he born?
d   Where does he live now?
e   Who does he live with?
f   What does his father do?
g   How was he different when he was very young?
h   What does he do in the evening?
i   Can his father speak English?
j   Does he have any friends?
k   What does he do in his free time?

Check your answers with your group.

Ivan Mirsky is thirteen and he is the number 13 chess player in the world.

He was born in Russia but now lives in America with his father, Vadim. They live in a one-room flat in Brooklyn. Ivan doesn't go to school and his father doesn't have a job. They practise chess problems all day, every day, morning, afternoon, and evening.

Ivan was different from a very young age: he could ride a bike when he was eighteen months old and read before he was two. He could play cards at three and the piano at four. When he was twelve, he was the under-20 chess champion of Russia.

His father can't speak English and can't play chess, either! Ivan translates for him. Vadim says, 'I know that I can't play chess, but I can still help Ivan. He and I don't have any friends – we don't want any friends. Other teenagers are boring! We don't like playing sports or watching TV. We live for chess!'

TWO TEENAGE GENIUSES

Jaya Rajah is fourteen, but he doesn't go to school. He studies medicine at New York University in a class of twenty-year-olds. Jaya was born in Madras in India but now lives in a house in New York with his mother, father, and brother. They can all speak English fluently. His father is a doctor.

Jaya was different from a very young age. He could count before he could say 'Mummy' or 'Daddy'. He could answer questions on calculus when he was five and do algebra when he was eight. Now he studies from 8.15 to 4.00 every day at the university. Then he studies at home with his father from 6.30 to 10.00 every evening. Jaya doesn't have any friends. He never goes out in the evenings, but he sometimes watches TV. He says, 'I live for one thing – I want to be a doctor before I am seventeen. Other children of my age are boring. They can't understand me.'

Speaking

1 Find a partner from the other group.
Discuss the answers again and tell your partner about the teenager in your text.

2 Now read the other text.
How many similarities and differences can you find?

> They both live in New York.

> Ivan lives with just his father, but Jaya lives with his parents and his brother.

3 What do you think?
a Are Ivan and Jaya happy?
b Are friends important? Why?

Roleplay

Work in pairs.
Student A is a journalist, Student B is Ivan or Jaya.
Ask and answer questions. Use the questions in the Comprehension Check to help you prepare the interview.

> Hello, Ivan! Can I ask you one or two questions?

> Yes, of course.

> First of all, how old are you?

> I'm thirteen.

● VOCABULARY AND PRONUNCIATION

Words that sound the same

1 Look at the sentences. What do you notice about the underlined words?
I have a black eye.
No, he doesn't know the answer.

2 Find the words in B that have the same pronunciation as the words in A.
Check the meaning of new words in your dictionary.

A
hear see write
eye there for
know by knows
wear son hour
meat cheque too

B
right no check
where buy I
nose two sea
four meet their
our here sun

3 Each sentence has two words with the wrong spelling.
Correct the spelling mistakes.

a I can here you, but I can't sea you.
b Their are three bedrooms in hour house.
c John nose wear Jill lives.
d My sun lives near the see.
e Don't where that hat when you meat the Queen!
f They no Anna two.
g You were write. Sally and Peter don't eat meet.
h There daughter could right when she was three.
i I want to by too new pens.
j Cheque that your answers are write.

4 Here are some spellings in phonetics. Write the two words which sound the same.

a /nəʊz/ _____ _____
b /sʌn/ _____ _____
c /miːt/ _____ _____
d /tʃek/ _____ _____
e /tuː/ _____ _____
f /raɪt/ _____ _____
g /hɪə/ _____ _____
h /weə/ _____ _____

● EVERYDAY ENGLISH

At the airport

1 **T 34a** Listen to the airport announcements and complete the chart.

FLIGHT NUMBER	●	DESTINATION	GATE NUMBER	● ●	REMARK
B A 5 1 6	●	G E N E V A	1 4	● ●	LAST CALL
S K	●			● ●	LAST CALL
A F	●			● ●	DELAYED 30 mins
L H	●			● ●	NOW BOARDING
V S	●			● ●	NOW BOARDING

2 Where do you go first when you travel by plane? Put these places in the correct order. Write 1-5 on the left.

___ passport control   ___
___ baggage reclaim   ___
1 the check-in desk   ___
___ the plane   ___
___ the arrival hall   ___
___ the departure lounge   **a**

3 **T 34b** Read and listen to the conversations. Where are they? Write the letter next to the correct place on the right in Exercise 2.

a A Ah! … BA 476 to Madrid. That's our flight.
   B Was it gate 4 or 14?
   A I couldn't hear. I think it was 4.
   B Ssssh! There it is again. It *is* gate 4.
   A OK. Come on!

b A Can I see your passport, please?
   B Yes, of course. Here you are.
   A Thank you very much. That's fine.

c A Can I have your ticket, please?
   B Yes, of course. Here you are.
   A Do you have just one suitcase?
   B Yes. This bag is hand luggage.
   A That's fine. Smoking or non-smoking?
   B Non-smoking, please. Oh ... and can I have a seat next to the window?
   A Yes, that's OK. Here's your boarding pass. Have a nice flight!

d A Can I have your tray please, madam?
   B Yes. Here you are.
   A Thank you. And can you fasten your seat belt? We land in ten minutes.
   B Yes, of course.

e A Excuse me. I think that's my suitcase.
   B I'm sorry. My suitcase is red, too.
   A Is this yours?
   B Yes, it is. Thank you very much.

f A Hello. Are you Marie-Thérèse Scherer from Switzerland?
   B Yes, I am. Are you Mr and Mrs Barnes?
   A Yes, we are. Welcome to England, Marie-Thérèse. Was your flight good?
   B Yes, it was, but I don't like flying.
   C Never mind. You're here safely now. Come on, the car's outside.

4 Read the conversations again carefully. Who are the people?

5 **T 34c** Close your books.
Listen to some of the lines from the conversations. There is a pause after each one for you to respond. You can use the ideas from the conversations in the book or your own ideas.

6 Work in groups of two or three.
Think of some roleplays in an airport or on a plane.
Choose a place and some characters.
You can be travellers from different countries, pilots, customs officers ...!

GRAMMAR SUMMARY

can/can't

Can and *can't* have the same form in all persons. There is no *do* or *does*.
Can is followed by the infinitive (without *to*).

could/couldn't

Could is the past of *can*. *Could* and *couldn't* have the same form in all persons.
Could is followed by the infinitive (without *to*).

Positive

I You He/She/It We They	can could	swim.

Negative

I You He/She/It We They	can't couldn't	dance.

NOT He ~~doesn't can~~ dance.

Question

What	can could	I you he/she/it we they	do?

Yes/No questions

Can Could	you she they etc.	drive? cook?

Short answers

No, I can't./No, we couldn't.
Yes, she can/could.
Yes, they can/could.

NOT ~~Do you can~~ drive?

was/were

Was/were is the past of *am/is/are*.

Positive

I She/He/It	was	in Paris yesterday.
We You They	were	in England last year.

Negative

I He/She/It	wasn't	at school yesterday.
We You They	weren't	at the party last night.

Question

Where	was	I? he/she/it?
	were	we? you? they?

Yes/No questions

Was	he she	at work?
Were	you they etc.	at home?

Short answers

No, he wasn't.
Yes, she was.

Yes, I was./Yes, we were.
No, they weren't.

was born

Where	was	she he	born?
	were	you they etc.	

I was born in Manchester in 1970. NOT I ~~am born~~ in 1970.

Prepositions

They were **in** England **in** 1980.
I was **at** a party.
We land **in** ten minutes.
He studies **from** 8.15 **to** 4.00.

Study the Word List for this unit on page 124.

UNIT 7

Past Simple (1) – Special occasions

Then and now

PRESENTATION (1)

Regular verbs

1   Check the meaning of these verbs.

earn	move (house)	retire	die

2   Look at the photograph and read text A about Ellen Peel.

A ────────

*Ellen Peel is over ninety
years old. She lives in a
village in the country with
her five cats. She is not
married, but she loves
children. She is very happy,
but she can remember
times when her life was
difficult. She often thinks
about her past.*

3   **T 35a**   Read and listen to text B.

B ────────

*Ellen's father died in the
war in 1915 and her
mother died a year later.
Ellen was twelve years
old. Immediately she
started work as a
housemaid with a rich
family in London.*

Now answer the Grammar
questions.

● Grammar questions

–   Which text is about the present?
    Which is about the past?
–   Find an example of the past of *is*.
    What are the last two letters of the other verbs
    in text B?
–   Complete the rule.
    To form the Past Simple of regular verbs, add _____ to
    the infinitive.

4   **T 35b**   Read and listen to text C.
    Fill in the gaps. Use the Past Simple form of the verbs in
    the box.

love   stay   retire   look   work   move   earn   clean   like

C ────────

*She _____ from 5.30 in the morning until 9.00 at night.
She _____ all the rooms in the house before breakfast. She
_____ £25 a year.
In 1921 she _____ to another family. She _____ her new
job because she _____ after the children. There were five
children, four sons and
one daughter.
She _____ them,
especially the baby,
Robert. She _____
with that family for
twenty years. Ellen
never married. She just
looked after other
people's children until
she _____ when she
was seventy years old.*

47

Practice

1 Grammar

Match a line in A with a line in B. Put the verb in B into the Past Simple.

A	B
a I was only twelve years old	because I _____ (work) very long hours.
b I was always tired in my first job	but in 1920 I _____ (live) in London.
c I started work at 5.30 in the morning	when my mother _____ (die) and I _____ (start) work.
d Now I live in a village,	but I _____ (love) Robert especially.
e Now I look after my five cats.	and I _____ (finish) at 9.00 in the evening.
f I loved all the children,	In the 1920s I _____ (look) after five children.
g Robert's over seventy now and I still see him.	He _____ (visit) me just last month.

2 Listening and pronunciation

1 **T 36a** Listen to Ellen and check your answers.

2 **T 36b** The past tense ending -ed has three different pronunciations. Listen and put the verbs in the correct columns.

/t/	/d/	/ɪd/
_____	_____	_____
_____	_____	_____
_____	_____	
_____	_____	
	_____	
	_____	

Practise saying the verbs.

PRESENTATION (2)

Questions and negatives

1 Read about Queen Victoria. Ask your teacher the questions below the text to find the missing information.

Queen Victoria was born in _____ (?) in 1819 and she died in _____(?). She was Queen of the United Kingdom for nearly sixty-four years.

Her father died when she was _____(?) and she was Queen from 1837 to 1901. She didn't have any brothers or sisters. She married Prince Albert in _____(?) and they lived in _____(?) with their _____(?) children.

When did she die?
When did she marry Prince Albert?
How many children did they have?
Where was she born?
Where did they live?
When did her father die?

2 **T 37** Listen and practise saying the questions.

⚠️

> 1 *Did* is the past of *do* and *does*. We use *did* to form a question about the past.
>
> Where **do** you work (now)?   Where **does** she live (now)?
> Where **did** you work in 1980?   Where **did** she live in 1950?
>
> 2 We use *didn't* to form a negative.
>
> She **didn't** have any brothers or sisters.

● Grammar question

Complete the rule.
To form questions in the Past Simple, we use the auxiliary

verb _____ and the _____ (without *to*).

Practice

1 Speaking

Work in pairs. Your teacher will give you some more information about Queen Victoria and Prince Albert, but you don't have the same information as your partner. Ask and answer questions to complete the information.

Example

Student A	**Student B**
Prince Albert was German and they married in (*Where?*) in 1840.	Prince Albert was (*What nationality?*) and they married in London in 1840.

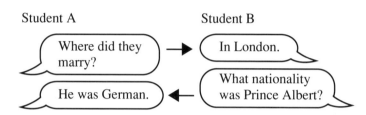

Student A — Where did they marry? → Student B — In London.

What nationality was Prince Albert? → He was German.

2 Grammar and speaking

1 Put *did*, *was*, or *were* into the gaps.

  a Where _____ you born? Where _____ your mother born?

  b When _____ you start school?

  c How many schools _____ you go to?

  d What _____ your favourite subject?

  e Where _____ you live when you _____ a child?

  f _____ you live in a house or a flat?

2 Stand up!
  Ask two or three students the questions in Exercise 1.

3 Tell the class some of the information you learned.

Enrico was born in ...   He started school ...   His mother ...

PRESENTATION (3)

Irregular verbs

1 Three of the verbs in the box are regular. Which are they? The others are irregular. Check the meanings in your dictionary and write in the Past Simple forms of all the verbs. There is a list of irregular verbs on page 127.

have	_____	come	_____	work	_____	go	_____
leave	_____	hate	_____	get	_____	give	_____
become	_____	write	_____	change	_____	win	_____
lose	_____	find	_____	buy	_____	sell	_____

---

2 **T 38** Listen and repeat the Past Simple verb forms.

3 How old were you in 1980? What can you remember about the 1980s?
  Think about your life, sport, and politics.

4 **T 39** Listen to Kevin talking about the 1980s.

ABOUT HIM

a He _____ school in 1982. He was unemployed, but then he _____ a job in an office. He _____ computer software.

b His parents _____ a video recorder in 1985 and his brother _____ a video computer game for his birthday in 1986.

c Kevin _____ his job in 1990.

SPORT

d The USSR _____ _____ to the Olympics in 1984, but both the United States and the USSR _____ to Seoul in 1988.

e Argentina _____ the World Cup in 1986.

POLITICS

f Reagan _____ the US president in 1981, Gorbachev _____ the world *glasnost* and *perestroika*, and the Berlin Wall _____ down in 1989.

Complete the sentences. Listen again and check.

5 Here are the answers to some questions about the listening text. Write the questions.

Example
In 1982.
When did Kevin leave school?

  a Computer software.   d In 1990.
  b In 1985.   e In 1986.
  c A video computer game.   f In 1989.

49

Practice

1 Speaking

1 Look at the past time expressions.

| last | night
Monday
week
month
year | yesterday | morning
afternoon
evening |

We cannot say ~~last evening~~ or ~~last afternoon~~.

2 Work in pairs. Ask and answer questions with *When did you last ...?* Ask one more question each time.

Example
have a holiday

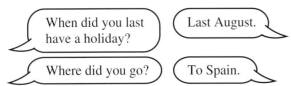

When did you last have a holiday? — Last August.

Where did you go? — To Spain.

a see a video
b go shopping
c give someone a kiss
d take a photograph
e go to a party
f lose something
g write a letter
h get a present
i have dinner in a restaurant

Tell the class some things you learned about your partner.

Keiko had a holiday last August and she went to Spain.

2 Choosing the correct sentence

One sentence has a mistake. Choose the correct sentence. Put ✔ and ✗.

1 a He bought some new shoes.
  b He buyed some new shoes.
2 a Where did you go yesterday?
  b Where you went yesterday?
3 a You see Jane last week?
  b Did you see Jane last week?
4 a Did she found a job?
  b Did she find a job?
5 a We didn't enjoyed the film.
  b We didn't enjoy the film.
6 a I didn't go out yesterday evening.
  b I didn't go out last evening.
7 a I was to school for the first time when I was six.
  b I went to school for the first time when I was six.
8 a Last night I have dinner with friends.
  b Last night I had dinner with friends.

READING

Pre-reading task

1 Do you know any British or American writers? What do you know about them?

2 Do you know any books by Charles Dickens? When did he live? Do you know anything about Victorian England?

3 Check the meaning of these words in your dictionary. Put one of the words into each gap.

novelist (*n*)	clerk (*n*)	debt (*n*)	prison (*n*)
factory (*n*)	popular (*adj*)	experience (*n*)	
lawcourt (*n*)	abroad (*adv*)	successful (*adj*)	

a All the students like Anna. She's a very _____ girl.
b My mother writes books, but she isn't a famous _____ .
c Alan started work in a bank last week. He's a _____ .
d He has ten clothes shops. He's a rich, _____ businessman.
e I don't like borrowing money. I hate being in _____ .
f I live near a very big _____ that makes cars.
g I went round the world for a year. It was a wonderful _____ .
h She often goes _____ in her job, sometimes to Hong Kong, sometimes to Canada.

Reading

Read the text about the life of Charles Dickens.

Comprehension check

1 Are the sentences true (✔) or false (✗)? Correct the false sentences.

a Charles Dickens wrote novels.
b He wrote only about the lives of rich and famous people.
c His father had a good job.
d Charles never went to school.
e He went to prison when he was eleven.
f His first job was in a factory.
g He became a journalist when he was fifteen.
h He never married.

Charles Dickens (1812-1870)

Charles Dickens is one of the greatest novelists in the English language. He wrote about the real world of Victorian England and many of his characters were not rich, middle-class ladies and gentlemen, but poor and hungry people.

DICKENS THE CHILD

His family lived in London. His father was a clerk in an office. It was a good job, but he always spent more money than he earned and he was often in debt. There were eight children in the family, so life was hard.

Charles went to school and his teachers thought he was very clever. But suddenly, when he was only eleven, his father went to prison for his debts and the family went, too. Only Charles didn't go to prison. He went to work in a factory, where he washed bottles. He

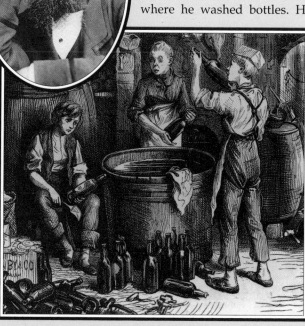

worked ten hours a day and earned six shillings (30p) a week. Every night, after work, he walked four miles back to his room. Charles hated it and never forgot the experience. He used it in many novels, especially *David Copperfield* and *Oliver Twist*.

DICKENS THE WRITER

When he was sixteen, he started work for a newspaper. He visited law courts and the Houses of Parliament. Soon he was one of the *Morning Chronicle*'s best journalists. He also wrote short stories for magazines. These were funny descriptions of people that he met. Dickens' characters were full of colour and life – good people were very, very good and bad people were horrible. His books became popular in many countries

and he spent a lot of time abroad, in America, Italy, and Switzerland.

DICKENS THE MAN

Dickens had ten children, but he didn't have a happy family life. He was successful in his work but not at home, and his wife left him. He never stopped writing and travelling, and he died very suddenly in 1870.

2 Answer the questions.

a How old was Dickens when he died?
b How many brothers and sisters did he have?
c Was he good at school?
d Why did he leave school when he was eleven?
e Who was in prison?
f What did Charles do in his first job?
g What was his next job?
h Was he happy at home?
i When did he stop writing?

Writing

Write about your past. Use these ideas to help you.

Born	Parents	School	Free time	First job
when?	work?	like?	sports?	what?
where?	live?	not like?	hobbies?	when?
				earn?

● VOCABULARY AND PRONUNCIATON

Silent letters

1 English spelling is not phonetic, so there are many silent letters in English words.

Here are some words from the text about Charles Dickens. Practise saying them.

de**b**t	/det/	ei**gh**t	/eɪt/
hard	/hɑːd/	thou**gh**t	/θɔːt/

Cross out the silent letters in these words.

Example
ni~~gh~~t

a	walk	d	writer	g	work	j	half
b	listen	e	autumn	h	short	k	foreign
c	know	f	farm	i	high	l	daughter

T 40a Listen and check. Practise saying the words.

2 Here are some of the words from Exercise 1 in phonetics. Write the words.

Example
/wɔːk/ = *walk*

a	/wɜːk/ _____	d	/ɔːtəm/ _____
b	/fɑːm/ _____	e	/raɪtə/ _____
c	/lɪsən/ _____	f	/dɔːtə/ _____

3 Here are some other words in phonetics. Write the words. Be careful! They all have silent letters.

a	/tɔːk/ _____	f	/waɪt/ _____
b	/bɔːn/ _____	g	/naɪf/ _____
c	/bɔːt/ _____	h	/rɒŋ/ _____
d	/wɜːld/ _____	i	/kʌbəd/ _____
e	/ɑːnsə/ _____	j	/krɪsməs/ _____

T 40b Listen and practise saying the words.

● EVERYDAY ENGLISH

Special occasions

1 Look at the list of days. Which are special? Check the meaning of new words in your dictionary. Match the special days with the photographs and objects.

```
Thursday
birthday
Monday
wedding day
Christmas Day
yesterday
New Year's Eve
Easter Day
tomorrow
Mother's Day
today
Valentine's Day
Friday
```

Look at the photographs again. Do you have the same customs in your country?

2 Complete the conversations.

a A Ugh! Work again! I hate _____ !
  B Me, too. Did you have a nice weekend?
  A Yes. It was wonderful.

b Happy _____ to you.
  Happy _____ to you.
  Happy _____ , dear Katie.
  Happy _____ to you.

c A How many _____ eggs did you get?
  B Six. What about you?
  A Five. I had them all on _____ morning before lunch.
  B Did you?
  A And then I was sick!
  B Ugh!

Dear Mum

Happy Mother's Day

Lots of Love from

Kate x x

d A Congratulations!
   B Oh … thank you very much.
   A When's the happy day?
   B Pardon?
   A Your _____ day. When is it?
   B Oh! We're not sure yet. Some time in June, probably.

e A Hello! Merry _____ , everyone!
   B Merry _____ ! Come in, come in. It's so cold outside.

f A Wonderful! It's _____ !
   B Yes. Have a nice weekend!
   A Same to you.

T 41a Listen and check. In pairs, practise the conversations.

3 **T 41b** Listen and answer.

GRAMMAR SUMMARY

Past Simple

The form of the Past Simple is the same in all persons.

Positive

I You He/She/It We They	went moved	to London in 1985.

Negative

We use *didn't* + infinitive (without *to*) in all persons.

I You He/She/It We They	didn't	go move	to London.

Question

We use *did* + infinitive (without *to*) in all persons.

When Where	did	I you he/she/it we they	go?

Yes/No questions

Did	you she they etc.	like	the film? the family?

Short answers

No, I didn't./No, we didn't.
Yes, she did.
No, they didn't.

Remember the list of irregular verbs on page 127.

Time expressions

last	night Saturday week month year	yesterday	morning afternoon evening

Prepositions

I often think **about** you.
I have a shower **before** breakfast.
I am always **in** debt.
Write **about** when you were young.
The box is full **of** books.

Study the Word List for this unit on page 124.

UNIT 8

Past Simple (2) – Time expressions – Ordinals and dates

How things began

PRESENTATION (1)

Negatives and *ago*

1 What century is it now? What was the last century? What year is it now? What year was it one hundred years ago?

2 Look at the photographs. Complete the questions with the correct verb from the box.

drive	eat	listen to	make	write	ride
take	travel (× 2)	use	watch	wear	

3 Ask and answer questions.

> Did people drive cars one hundred years ago?

> Yes, I think they did.

> I'm not sure.

> No, they didn't.

4 Say the things people did and the things people didn't do.

> People rode bikes.

> They didn't watch TV.

5 Listen! Your teacher knows the answers and the correct dates.

● Grammar question

Complete the rule.
To form the negative in the Past Simple, we use the auxiliary verb _____ + _____ and the _____ (without *to*).

ONE HUNDRED YEARS AGO DID PEOPLE...

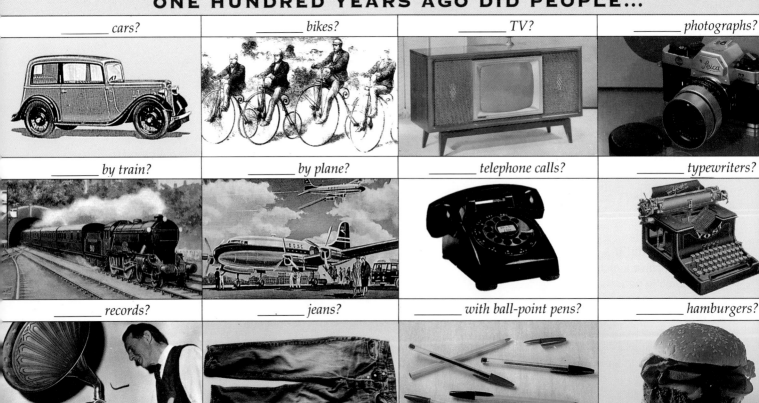

_____ cars?

_____ bikes?

_____ TV?

_____ photographs?

_____ by train?

_____ by plane?

_____ telephone calls?

_____ typewriters?

_____ records?

_____ jeans?

_____ with ball-point pens?

_____ hamburgers?

Practice

1 Reading and listening

1 Read the three texts. Check the meaning of new words in your dictionary.
There are three mistakes in each text. Can you find any of them?

2 **T 42** Listen and correct the mistakes.

> He didn't make the first hamburgers in 1985.
> He made them in 1895.

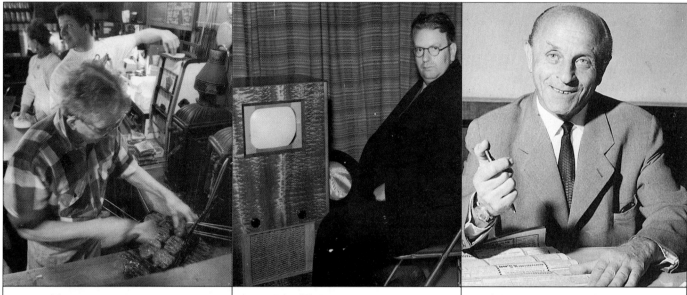

THE HAMBURGER	TELEVISION	THE BALL-POINT PEN
An American chef from Connecticut, Louis Lassen, made and sold the first hamburgers in 1985. He called them hamburgers because sailors from Hamburg in Germany gave him the recipe. Teachers from Yale University and businessmen loved them and bought them. Kenneth Lassen, Louis' son, still sells hamburgers in Connecticut.	A Scotsman, John Logie Baird, transmitted the first television picture on 25 October, 1825. The first thing on television was a cat from the office next to Baird's workroom in London. In 1927 Baird sent pictures from London to Glasgow. In 1928 he sent pictures to Paris and also produced the first colour TV pictures.	A Hungarian, Laszlo Biro, made the first ball-point pen in 1838. In 1944 the American Army bought thirty thousand because soldiers could write with them outside in the rain. At the end of the war 'Biros' quickly became very popular all over the world. In 1948 a shop in New York sold ten on one day.

2 Listening and pronunciation

1 **T 43** Read and listen to the conversations. Listen carefully to the intonation.

> Did you know that Marco Polo brought spaghetti back from China?

> Really? He didn't! That's incredible!

> Well, it's true!

> Did you know that Napoleon was afraid of cats?

> He wasn't! I don't believe it!

> Well, it's true!

2 Work in pairs.
Your teacher will give you two different lists of more incredible information!

Student A   Give the information, beginning *Did you know that ...?*
Student B   Make a reply.

Then change!

PRESENTATION (2)

Time expressions

How many correct time expressions can you make?

in on at	the twentieth century 1924 winter September 10 October weekends Christmas day Saturday Sunday evening the evening seven o'clock

Practice

1 Grammar and speaking

Ask and answer questions with *when*. Use a time expression and *ago* in the answer.

> When did you get up?

> At seven o'clock. Three hours ago.

> When did this term start?

> In September. Two months ago.

a   ... have breakfast?
b   ... arrive at school?
c   ... start learning English?
d   ... start this school?
e   ... first travel by plane?
f   ... last have a holiday?
g   ... last eat a hamburger?
h   ... learn to ride a bicycle?
i   ... your parents marry?
j   ... Shakespeare die?

2 Listening and speaking

1   What is the Past Simple of these verbs?

> break into   steal   eat   drink   feel   fall   wake up

2   **T 44**   Look at the pictures about a burglar and listen. It's a true story!

Complete the sentences with verbs from the box and your own ideas.
Don't write! Practise saying the story until you can remember it.

Picture 1
On 1 June 1992, a French burglar ... a house ... He ... living room and ...

Picture 2
Then ... kitchen. He opened ... cheese.

Picture 3
... hungry, so ... Next ... champagne.

Picture 4
... thirsty, so ... Then ... felt ...

Picture 5
... upstairs for ..., but ... tired ... fell ...

Picture 6
When ... the next ..., there were ... bed!

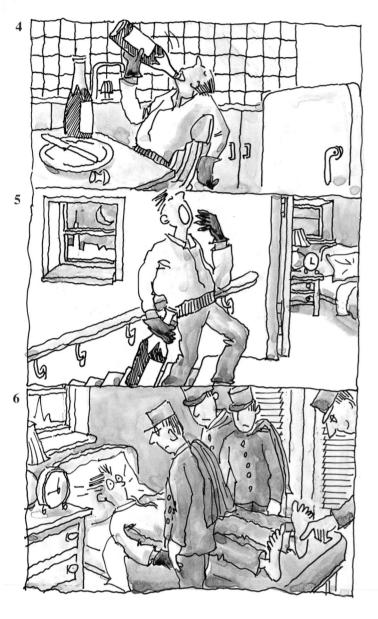

4

5

6

3 Complete the questions about the story.

Example
When *did he break into* the house?
On 1 June, 1992.

a How many pictures _____ ?
   Two.
b What _____ see _____ ?
   Some cheese.
c How _____ bottles _____ ?
   Two.
d Why _____ upstairs?
   Because he wanted a rest.
e When _____ up?
   Next morning.
f How many _____ ?
   Four.

4 Write the story for homework!

● VOCABULARY AND PRONUNCIATON

Odd one out

1 Which word is the odd one out? Why?

Example
orange   apple   ~~chicken~~   banana

> Chicken is the odd one out because it's an animal.
> The others are kinds of fruit.

Check the meaning of new words in your dictionary.

a camera	stereo	photograph	computer
b recipe	cake	bread	biscuit
c met	laughed	wrote	spoke
d fall in love	get married	get engaged	be retired
e pink	yellow	warm	blue
f war	sailor	soldier	pilot
g hair	voice	eyes	hand
h century	clock	season	month
i shy	nervous	angry	hungry
j fridge	dishwasher	television	washing machine

2 Where is the stress on these words? Put them in the correct column.

photograph   machine   recipe   camera   engaged
dishwasher   century   computer   married

● • •	• ●	• ● •	● •

3 Here are some words in phonetics. Practise saying the words.

a /bred/   c /lɑːft/   e /heə/   g /æŋgrɪ/
b /bɪskɪt/   d /wɔː/   f /mærɪd/   h /hʌŋgrɪ/

4 Put one of the words from Exercise 1 into each gap.

a My American cousin was a _____ in the Vietnam war.
b My daughter doesn't like parties because she's very _____ .
c He took a lovely _____ of the baby.
d They _____ when I told them the joke.
e Can I have that _____ for chocolate cake? It was wonderful.
f I _____ to our neighbour, Mrs Jones, today. She said she was fine.
g She's a very good singer. She has a beautiful _____ .
h 'How did you feel before the exam?' 'Very _____ .'
i I broke my father's camera yesterday. He was very _____ .

OLIVER AND WENDY MINT ▲

HOW ♥ *we* MET

▼ TREVOR AND ASTRID RICHARDS

● LISTENING AND SPEAKING

Pre-listening task

1 Put the sentences in order. There is more than one answer!

____ They got married.

____ They fell in love.

____ Jane and Roger met at a party.

____ He liked her before she liked him.

____ They have two children.

____ They went out together for a long time.

____ They wrote love letters.

2 Are you married? How did you meet your husband/wife? When did your parents meet? Where?

3 Look at the photographs of two couples. How old are they? What jobs do they do?

4 Check the meaning of new verbs in your dictionary. What is the past tense form of each verb?

| hear think wait smile ring tell forget speak laugh |

Listening

T 45 Divide into two groups.

Group A Listen to Wendy Mint.
Group B Listen to Trevor Richards.

Answer the questions about your couple.

Comprehension check

a When did they meet?
b How did they meet?
c What is his job?
d Was he at work when they met?
e What did he/she like about him/her?
f Are they both English?
g Who is shy?
h Wendy talks about a restaurant.
  Trevor talks about a cake. Why?
i When did they get married?
j Do they work together?
k Do they have any children?

Speaking

1 Find a partner from the other group. Discuss the answers and compare information.
2 Imagine that you are Oliver or Astrid. Tell the story of how you met your wife/husband.

● EVERYDAY ENGLISH

1 Ordinals

1 Write the correct word next to the numbers.

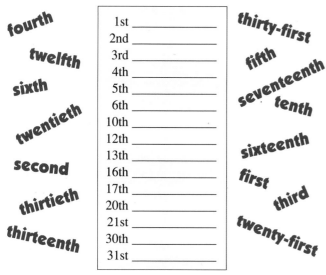

fourth *twelfth* *sixth* *twentieth* *second* *thirtieth* *thirteenth*

thirty-first *fifth* *seventeenth* *tenth* *sixteenth* *first* *third* *twenty-first*

| 1st _____ |
| 2nd _____ |
| 3rd _____ |
| 4th _____ |
| 5th _____ |
| 6th _____ |
| 10th _____ |
| 12th _____ |
| 13th _____ |
| 16th _____ |
| 17th _____ |
| 20th _____ |
| 21st _____ |
| 30th _____ |
| 31st _____ |

T 46a Listen and practise saying the ordinals.

2 Ask and answer questions about the months of the year.

Which is the first month?   January.

Which is the ninth month?   September.

2 Dates

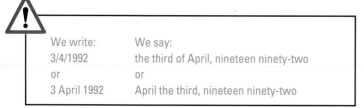

We write:	We say:
3/4/1992	the third of April, nineteen ninety-two
or	or
3 April 1992	April the third, nineteen ninety-two

Practise saying these dates:

1 April   2 March   17 September   19 November   23 June
15/7/67   29/2/76   19/12/83   3/10/70   31/5/93

T 46b Listen and check.

2 **T 46c** Listen and write the seven dates you hear.

3 Work in pairs. Ask and answer these questions.

a What's the date today?
b When did this school term start? When does it end?
c When's Christmas Day?
d When's Valentine's Day?
e When's Mothers' Day this year?
f When's American Independence Day?
g What century is it now?
h What are the dates of public holidays in your country?
i When were you born?
j When's your birthday?

GRAMMAR SUMMARY

Past Simple

Negative
Negatives in the Past Simple are the same in all persons.

| I
You
She
We
They
etc. | didn't | go out | last night. |

ago

| I went to the States | ten years
two weeks
a month | ago. |

Time expressions

in	the twentieth century 1924 winter/summer the evening/the morning September
on	10 October Christmas Day Saturday Sunday evening
at	seven o'clock weekends

Prepositions

I phoned him **at** the end **of** the programme.
My birthday is **on** the tenth **of** October.
Can I ask a question **about** your country?
She fell **in** love **with** his voice.

Study the Word List for this unit on page 125.

59

STOP AND CHECK

Units 5–8

1 Correcting the mistakes

Each sentence has a mistake. Find it and correct it!

Example
Where ~~you live~~?   *Where do you live?*

a   My brother go to university.
b   English is a language international.
c   I don't like swim.
d   I arrive at Heathrow airport at ten o'clock last night.
e   She could to speak three languages when she was ten.
f   Where did you went last night?
g   I saw the wife of Jeremy at the shops.
h   I don't can go out because I have a lot of homework.
i   In the kitchen is a table.
j   I was to the cinema last weekend.
k   My children like they're school very much.
l   I buyed a new video.
m   Did you watch the football on TV last evening?
n   Italian people is very artistic.
o   I like cities because I can to go to the theatre.

15

2 *can/could/was/were (not)*

Put a verb from the box into each gap.

| can/can't   could/couldn't   was/wasn't   were/weren't |

Example
I *can't* drive. I'm only 14 years old.

a   Our teacher _____ at school last week because she
    _____ ill.

b   Leonardo _____ a student in Florence. He _____
    draw, write music, and design buildings.

c   We _____ see the Mona Lisa in the Louvre in Paris.

d   'Where _____ you last night? You _____ at home.

    I phoned you, but there _____ no answer.'

    'I _____ get into my flat because I lost my keys. I

    _____ at a friend's house.'

10

3 Irregular verbs

Write the Past Simple form of these irregular verbs.

a   give   _____   f   make   _____
b   leave _____   g   break _____
c   sell   _____   h   meet   _____
d   speak _____   i   win   _____
e   lose   _____   j   take   _____

10

4 Past Simple

Fill in the gaps with the Past Simple form of the verbs in brackets. There are regular and irregular verbs.

Example
Leonardo da Vinci __*lived*__ (live) in Italy in the fifteenth and sixteenth centuries.

He was a student in Florence, where he (a) _____ (study) painting, sculpture, and design. He (b) _____ (begin) a lot of paintings, but he (c) _____ (not finish) many of them. His picture of the Mona Lisa is the most famous portrait in the world.

Leonardo (d) _____ (be) interested in many things. He (e) _____ (want) to know about everything he saw. He examined the human body. He (f) _____ (think) that the sun (g) _____ (not go) round the earth. He (h) _____ (write) music. He designed a flying machine 400 years before the first one flew. Many people

(i) _____ (not understand) his ideas. It is difficult to think that one man (j) _____ (can) do so much.

20

60

5 *a/an* or nothing?

Some of the sentences need *a* or *an*. Some of the
sentences are correct. Put *a/an* or ✔.

Examples
He has ~~good job~~.   *He has a good job.*
I don't like cheese.   ✔

a   I have toast for breakfast. _____

b   My sister works in office. _____

c   Do you like Indian food? _____

d   Is there Indian restaurant
    near here?   _____

e   Have nice weekend!   _____

f   There's good library near
    my house.   _____

g   Meat is expensive.   _____

h   My grandfather is
    engineer.   _____ **16**

6 some/any/a/an

Put *some*, *any*, *a*, or *an* into each gap.

Example
Heathrow is ___*an*___ international airport.

a   Did Charles Dickens have _____ children?

b   I bought _____ newspaper and _____ magazines.

c   Jane lives in _____ old house in France.

d   There are _____ trees in my garden, but there aren't
    _____ flowers.

e   Do you have _____ books by Gabriel García
    Márquez?

f   There are _____ letters for you on the table. **8**

7 Vocabulary – connections

Match a line in A with a line in B.

Example
Easter Day – egg

A	B
Easter Day	sun
cupboard	war
wallet	borrow
library	kitchen
check-in desk	egg
smell	wedding
Welcome to Britain!	luggage
son	chef
Congratulations!	arrival hall
recipe	nose
soldier	money

11

8 Vocabulary – opposites

Match a word in A with its opposite in B.

Example
wonderful – horrible

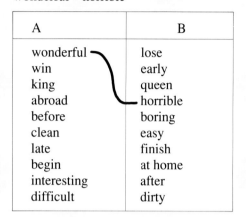

A	B
wonderful	lose
win	early
king	queen
abroad	horrible
before	boring
clean	easy
late	finish
begin	at home
interesting	after
difficult	dirty

10

Total **100**

TRANSLATE

Translate the sentences into your language. Translate the
ideas, not word by word.

1   Is there a chemist's near here?

    _____

2   There are two books on the table.

    _____

3   There are some flowers in the living room.

    _____

4   Are there any glasses?

    _____

5   I can type, but I can't spell.

    _____

6   I couldn't go to the party last night.

    _____

7   I was ill.

    _____

8   Where were you born?

    _____

9   I was born in Mexico.

    _____

10 She started work when she was twelve.

    _____

11 He didn't like his first job.

    _____

12 Where did you go on holiday last year?

    _____

Tapescript section

UNIT 1

Tapescript 1a

A Hello. My name's Jenny. What's your name?
B Anna.
A Where are you from, Anna?
B I'm from New York.

Tapescript 1b

A Hello. My name's Thomas. What's your name?
B Johann.
A Where are you from, Johann?
B I'm from Berlin. Where are you from?
A I'm from Oxford.

Tapescript 2

My name's Mayumi Kimura, and I'm a student. I'm 19 years old. I'm not married. I have two brothers and a sister. I live in a flat in Osaka, Japan. I want to learn English because it's an international language.

Tapescript 3

France	Spain	Greece	
England	Egypt	Russia	
Brazil	Japan		
Germany	Mexico	Hungary	Italy

Tapescript 4

1 He's from Spain.
2 I'm sixteen.
3 Her name's Pat.
4 They're from Britain.
5 Where's she from?
6 He's a teacher in France.

Tapescript 5

a A Hello, Mary. How are you?
   B Fine, thank you. And you?
   A I'm OK, thanks.

b A Hi, Dave. How are you?
   B Not bad, thanks. And you?
   A Very well. How are the children?
   B They're fine.

c A Goodbye, Chris.
   B Goodbye, Anne. Have a nice evening.
   A Thanks, Chris. See you tomorrow.

Tapescript 6

a stamp   a bag   a map   a key
an apple   a postcard   a ticket   a notebook
an orange   a letter   a suitcase   a camera
a dictionary   an envelope   a newspaper
a magazine

Tapescript 7a

a	h	j	k		
b	c	d	e	g	p	t	v
f	l	m	n	s	x	z
i	y				
o					
q	u	w			
r					

Tapescript 7b

The alphabet song

a	b	c	d	e	f	g	h	i	j	k	l
m	n	o	p								
l	m	n	o	p	q	r	ɘ	t			
l	m	n	o	p	q	r	s	t			
u	v	w	x	y	z						

That is the English alphabet.

Tapescript 7c

name	N - A - M - E
sister	S - I - S - T - E - R
flat	F - L - A - T
student	S - T - U - D - E - N - T
doctor	D - O - C - T - O - R
house	H - O - U - S - E
letter	L - E - double T - E - R
married	M - A - double R - I - E - D
apple	A - double P - L - E
job	J - O - B

Tapescript 7d

A How do you spell your first name?
B J - A - M - E - S.
A How do you spell your surname?
B H - A - double R - I - S - O - N.
A James Harrison.
B That's right.

UNIT 2

Tapescript 8

Numbers

5 20 16 32 50 12

Phone numbers

791463   859 6 double 2   503 971
010 double 3 1 46 58 93 94

Tapescript 9

A What's her surname?
B Hopkins.
A What's her first name?
B Mary.
A Where's she from?
B England.
A What's her job?
B She's a journalist.

A What's her address?
B 35, North Street, Bristol.
A What's her phone number?
B 0272 478 2209.
A How old is she?
B Twenty-three.
A Is she married?
B No, she isn't.

Tapescript 10

This is a photo of Martin, his wife, and his children. His wife's name is Jennifer. She's a dentist. His daughter's name is Alison. She's twenty-three and she's a hairdresser. His son's name is Andy. He's nineteen and he's a student. Alison's boyfriend is a travel agent. His name is Joe.

Tapescript 11

a It's big.
b It's small.
c She's old.
d She's young.
e They're expensive.
f They're cheap.
g It's horrible.
h It's lovely.
i It's easy.
j It's difficult.
k They're old.
l They're new.
m They're hot.
n They're cold.
o It's right.
p It's wrong.

Tapescript 12a

Paola's letter to David
(see page 16)

Tapescript 12b

P = Paola   K = Kurt

1 P Hello. My name's Paola.
   K Hello, Paola. I'm Kurt.
   P Where are you from?
   K I'm from Switzerland. And you? Where are you from?
   P I'm from Rome.
   K Ah! I'm from Zurich.
   P Zurich is very beautiful.
   K Yes, it is.

T = ticket seller

2 P A ticket to Green Park, please.
   T Two pounds fifty.
   P One ... two ... and fifty p.
   T Thank you. Here's your ticket.
   P Thanks.

B = Peter Briscall   C = class

3 B Good morning!
   C Good morning!
      Good morning, Peter!
      Hello!
   B How are you today?
   C Fine.
      OK.
   B How are you, Paola?
   P I'm fine thank you, Peter. And you?
   B Very well! Now, the lesson today is ...

C = assistant in café   K = Kurt

4 C Yes?
   P A coffee, please.
   C Black or white?
   P Sorry?
   C Black or white? Milk?
   P Ah! Black, please. No milk.
   C Sixty p, please.
   P Thanks.
   P Urgh!! It's horrible!
   K English coffee is very bad!

C = Catherine   T = Thomas

5 C Is your teacher good, Paola?
   P Pardon?
   C Your teacher. At the school of English.
   P Ah! Yes! Peter.
   C Is he OK?
   P Yes. He's very nice. He's funny.
   T What's your dad's job, Paola?
   P Pardon? I ...
   T Your dad. What's his job?
   P My dad ...?
   C Say father, Thomas, not dad.
   T Ah, OK. What's your father's job, Paola?
   P Now I understand. My father's job, yes. Um ... He's a doctor, yes.
   T Ah, right!

Tapescript 13a

sandwiches	
a ham sandwich	£1.50
a cheese sandwich	£1.30
a tuna sandwich	£1.70
a chicken sandwich	£2.00
a piece of pizza	90p
a hamburger	£2.50
an ice-cream	80p
a cup of tea	
a cup of coffee	

a Coke
an orange juice
a mineral water

A How much is a cup of tea?
B 50p.
A How much is a cup of coffee?
B 70p.
A How much is a Coke?
B 60p.
A How much is an orange juice?
B 60p.
A How much is a mineral water?
B 80p.

Tapescript 13b

a A Hello.
  B Hello. Can I have a ham sandwich, please?
  A Here you are. Anything else?
  B No, thanks.
  A One pound fifty, please.
  B Thanks.
  A Thank you.

b A Hi.
  B Hello. Can I have a cheese sandwich, please?
  A Anything to drink?
  B Yes. A cup of tea, please.
  A OK. Here you are.
  B How much is that?
  A One pound eighty, please.
  B Thanks.

c A Good morning.
  B Morning.
  A Can I have a hamburger and a cup of coffee, please?
  B OK. Here you are.
  A Thanks. How much is that?
  B Three pounds twenty.
  A One, two, three pounds ... twenty p.
  B Thanks.
  A Thank you.

UNIT 3

Tapescript 14

Sister Mary
Hans Huser
(see page 19)

Tapescript 15a

A Where does Sister Mary come from?
B Ireland.
A What does she do?
B She's a teacher.
A Does she speak French?
B Yes, she does.
A Does she speak German?
B No, she doesn't.

Tapescript 15b

a A Where does Hans come from?
  B Switzerland.
b A What does he do?
  B He's a ski-instructor.
c A Does he speak French and German?
  B Yes, he does.
d A Does he speak Spanish?
  B No, he doesn't.

Tapescript 16a

1 Georges comes from Paris.
2 Georges lives in London.
3 He works in the centre of Paris.
4 In his free time he plays tennis.
5 Keiko comes from China.
6 She lives in Washington.
7 She speaks French and German.
8 She's married to an American.
9 Mark comes from England.
10 He works in Liverpool.
11 He speaks Italian.
12 In his free time he goes walking.

Tapescript 16b

1 She likes her job.
2 She loves walking.
3 She's married.
4 Does he have three children?
5 Where does he go?
6 She watches the television.

Tapescript 17

a A Good morning, sir. Can I see your ticket?
  B Yes, of course. Here you are.
  A Thank you. Maidstone next stop.
  B Thank you.

b A Good morning, boys and girls.
  B Good morning, Mr Garret.
  A Can I have your homework, please?
  B It's on your desk, Mr Garret.
  A Thank you.

c A Goodbye, Frank. Have a good journey!
  B Thank you very much.
  A See you next Monday.
  B Yes, of course. Goodbye!

d A Excuse me. Is this seat free?
  B Yes, it is.
  A Thank you. It's cold this evening.
  B It certainly is. And the sea's very black!

e A Hello darling! Are you tired?
  B Yes, I am. And cold.
  A Sit down and have a glass of wine.
  B Mmmm! Thank you. I'm hungry, too.

Tapescript 18a

It's five o'clock.   It's eight o'clock.   It's half past five.   It's half past eleven.
It's quarter past five.   It's quarter past two.   It's quarter to six.   It's quarter to nine.
It's five past five.   It's ten past five.   It's twenty past five.   It's twenty-five past five.
It's twenty-five to six.   It's twenty to six.   It's ten to six.   It's five to six.

Tapescript 18b

A Excuse me. Can you tell me the time, please?
B Yes, of course. It's six o' clock.
A Thanks.

A Excuse me. Can you tell me the time, please?
B I'm sorry. I don't know. I don't have a watch.

UNIT 4

Tapescript 19a

On Fridays I come home from the BBC at about 2.00 in the afternoon and I just relax. On Friday evenings I don't go out, but sometimes a friend comes for dinner. He or she brings the wine and I cook the meal. I love cooking! We listen to music or we just chat.
On Saturday mornings I get up at 9.00 and I go shopping. Then in the evenings I sometimes go to the theatre or the opera with a friend – I love opera! Then we eat in my favourite Chinese restaurant. On Sunday... Oh, on Sunday mornings I stay in bed late, I don't get up until 11.00! Sometimes in the afternoon I visit my sister. She lives in the country and has two children. I like playing with my niece and nephew, but I leave early because I go to bed at 8.00 on Sunday evenings!

Tapescript 19b

A Do you go out on Friday afternoons?
B No, I don't.
A What do you do?
B I just relax.
A Do you stay at home on Friday evenings?
B Yes, I do.
A What do you do?
B I cook dinner for friends.

Tapescript 20

1 What does he do on Sundays?
2 I stay at home on Thursday evenings.
3 He lives here.
4 I eat a lot.
5 Where do you go on Saturday evenings?
6 She likes cars.

Tapescript 21a

Mr and Mrs Forrester have a son and a daughter. The son lives at home, and the daughter is a student at university. Mr Forrester is a journalist. He works for *The Times*. He writes articles about restaurants. 'I love food!' he says.

Tapescript 21b

'Every spring the children go skiing, so my wife and I go to Paris on holiday. We stay in a hotel near the River Seine. We have breakfast in the hotel, but we have lunch in a restaurant. French food is delicious! We walk a lot, but sometimes we go by taxi. After four days we don't want to go home and go back to work.'

Tapescript 22a

Al Wheeler
Manuela da Silva
Toshi Suzuki
(see page 29)

Tapescript 22b

M = Manuela J = Jane F = Manuela's friends
P = Portuguese man
1 M Hello, everybody! This is my friend Jane, from England.
  F Hi!
    Hello!
    Hello, Jane!
  J Hello. Pleased to meet you.
  M Sit down here, Jane.
  J Thanks.
  P Do you like this music, Jane?
  J Mm. Is it American?
  P No, it's Brazilian jazz!
  M Come and have a drink, Jane ...

T = Toshi J = Ann Jones
2 T Mrs Jones! How do you do?
  J How do you do?

T Please come in. You're from our office in London, aren't you?
J Yes, that's right.
T Welcome to Tokyo! Do you like our headquarters here?
J Yes. It's very big. How many people work here?
T About six thousand people. Do you want to see our offices? ...

A = Al M = Mick (Scottish)

3 A What do you want to do today, Mick?
M Ooh, I don't know. What do you ...
A Well, do you like fishing?
M Yes. I sometimes go fishing in a river near my house in Scotland.
A Well, here it's different. This is a very big country. I go fishing on a lake. It's a hundred kilometres long!
M A hundred kilometres!
A Yeah! There are fish this big! Are you interested? Do you want to go?
M OK!
A Right. You want a fishing line ...

Tapescript 23

a A Excuse me!
   B Yes?
   A Do you have a light?
   B I'm sorry. I don't smoke.
   A That's OK.

b A I'm sorry I'm late. The traffic is bad today.
   B Don't worry. Come and sit down. We're on page 25.

c A Can I open the window? It's very hot in here.
   B Really? I'm quite cold.
   A OK. It doesn't matter.

d G Excuse me!
   H Can I help you?
   G Can I have a film for my camera?
   H How many exposures?
   G Pardon?
   H How many exposures?
   G What does *exposures* mean?
   H How many pictures? 24? 36?
   G Ah! Now I understand! 36, please.

UNIT 5

Tapescript 24

A Is there a stereo?   A Are there any books?
B Yes, there is.   B Yes, there are.
A Is there a clock?   A Are there any magazines?
B No, there isn't.   B No, there aren't.

Tapescript 25

Picture A
There are four pictures on the walls and a mirror. There are three people in the room, a man, a woman, and a girl. There's a lovely fire and the cat is in front of the fire, sleeping. There's a lamp near the window, and a clock on the wall near the mirror. There's a photo on the television and there are some newspapers on the floor near the television. There's a glass of beer on the table in front of the man. The television isn't on.

Picture B
There are two people in the room. There's a man on the sofa and a woman next to him. The cat's in front of the fire. There are four pictures on the walls.

There are two plants, one on the left of the fire and one on the right. On the table in front of the man there are some cups and some books and on the table next to the sofa there is a telephone.

Tapescript 26

It's a modern kitchen, nice and clean with a lot of cupboards. There's a washing machine, a fridge and a cooker, but there isn't a dishwasher. There are some lovely pictures on the walls, but there aren't any photographs. There's a radio near the cooker. There are some flowers, but there aren't any plants. On the table there are some apples and oranges. Ah! And there are some cups and plates next to the sink.

Tapescript 27

What's in my bag? Well, there's a newpaper – a French newspaper – and there's my dictionary. I have some pens, three, I think. There's a photo of my wife and a photo of my children. I have my notebook for vocabulary, of course. I write words in that every day. I have some keys, and that's all! I don't have any stamps and I don't have a bus ticket. Oh, and I have a letter, from my bank manager. He wants my money!

Tapescript 28

Anne-Marie
I live in a house in the country in Provence in the south of France. It's an old farmhouse, about five hundred years old, with very thick walls, so it's warm in winter and cool in summer, but it's difficult to look after because it's so old. There are three bedrooms, two quite big and one small, and they have wonderful views over the countryside. I have a garden where I grow flowers and vegetables. I live with my animals! I have two dogs and eight cats.

Harry
Where I live things are big. I live in Texas – that's the second biggest state in the USA – and I live with my wife and our four children. We have ten cars because we all like driving. Sometimes we drive 150 kilometres to go to a restaurant! Our house is three years old, and it's kind of big. There are fourteen or fifteen bedrooms, I don't know exactly, and outside there are two swimming pools and ... a golf course ... and some grass for my plane to land on.

Dave and Maggie
Maggie We have a small house in an area of Dublin called Donnybrook. It's quite a small house. There's a living room and a kitchen downstairs, and then two small bedrooms upstairs, but it's big enough for us. There's my husband and me, and our son, Thomas.
Dave The houses around here are about a hundred years old and people are very friendly. People don't want to move away, they want to live near their family, so my parents are very close...
Maggie ... and my mother lives next door! We have a small garden where Thomas plays, and I go out and have a chat with my mother!

Thanos
I live in a flat on the fourth floor. I live alone. There's a kitchen where I cook and eat, a living room with a balcony, and two small bedrooms. I live in Athina – you say Athens in English – but not in the centre of town because there are too many cars. It's a nice area. The shops aren't too far, and the flat is comfortable. It's about five years old, which I like. I don't like old buildings.

Tapescript 29

a A Excuse me! Is there a chemist's near here?
   B Yes. It's over there.
   A Thanks.

b A Excuse me! Is there a sports club near here?
   B Yes. It's in Queen Street. Take the second street on the right.
   A Thanks.

c A Excuse me! Is there a newsagent's near here?
   B Yes. There's one in Church Street next to the bank and there's one in Park Lane opposite the swimming pool.
   A Is that one far?
   B No. Just two minutes, that's all.

d A Is there a cinema near here?
   B Take the first left, and it's on the left, opposite the flower shop.
   A Thanks a lot.

UNIT 6

Tapescript 30a

a A Can you speak Japanese?
   B No, I can't.
b I can't hear you. The line's bad.
c A Can you use a word processor?
   B Yes, I can.
d I can't spell your name.
e Cats can see in the dark.
f She can type fifty words a minute.

Tapescript 30b

a I can type, but I can't spell.
b He can sing and he can dance.
c A Can you cook?
   B Yes, I can.
d They can ski, but they can't swim.
e We can read and we can write.
f A Can she drive?
   B No, she can't.

Tapescript 31

Sarah
Well, there are a lot of things I can't do! I can't draw and I can't drive a car, but I want to have lessons. I can ... I can type and I can use a word processor, because I have one at work and I use it all the time. What about sports? Mm. Well, I certainly can't ski, but I'm quite good at tennis, yes, I can play tennis. Well, I usually win when I play with my friends. And I can swim, of course. And I can cook. I think I'm a very good, well, no, just good ... a good cook! Now, then ... languages. I can speak French and German, I don't know any Italian at all, and I know about five words in Spanish – adios, mañana, paella – no, I can't speak Spanish! And I can't play any musical instruments, not the piano, the guitar, or anything.

Tapescript 32

A What day was it yesterday?
B It was Thursday.
A Where were you yesterday?
B I was at school.
A Were you at home yesterday?
B Yes, I was.
A The restaurant was cheap. But the food wasn't very good.

A Could you play the piano when you were six?
B No, I couldn't.

Tapescript 33

Sue Were you at Eve's party last Saturday?
Bill Yes, I was.
Sue Was it good?
Bill Well, it was OK.
Sue Were there many people?
Bill Yes, there were.
Sue Was Tom there?
Bill No, he wasn't. And where were you?
Sue Oh ... I couldn't go because I was at Adam's party! It was brilliant!

Tapescript 34a

This is flight information for today, 24 June. British Airways flight BA 516 to Geneva at gate 14, last call. Flight BA 516 to Geneva, last call, gate 14. Scandinavian Airlines flight SK 832 to Frankfurt at gate 7, last call. Flight SK 832 to Frankfurt, last call, gate 7. Air France flight AF 472 to Amsterdam is delayed thirty minutes. Flight AF 472 to Amsterdam, delayed thirty minutes. Lufthansa flight LH 309 to Miami, now boarding at gate 32. Flight LH 309 to Miami now boarding at gate 32. Virgin flight VS 876 to New York, now boarding at gate 20. Flight VS 876, now boarding at gate 20. Passengers are reminded to keep their luggage with them at all times. Thank you.

Tapescript 34b

At the airport
(see page 45)

Tapescript 34c

a Was it Gate 4 or 14?
b Can I see your passport, please?
c Smoking or non-smoking?
d Can I have your tray please, madam?
e Excuse me. I think that's my suitcase.
f Welcome to England! Was your flight good?

UNIT 7

Tapescript 35a

Text B
Ellen's father died in the war in 1915 and her mother died a year later. Ellen was twelve years old. Immediately she started work as a housemaid with a rich family in London.

Tapescript 35b

Text C
She worked from 5.30 in the morning until 9.00 at night. She cleaned all the rooms in the house before breakfast. She earned £25 a year.
In 1921 she moved to another family. She liked her new job because she looked after the children. There were five children, four sons and one daughter. She loved them, especially the baby, Robert. She stayed with that family for twenty years. Ellen never married. She just looked after other people's children until she retired when she was seventy years old.

Tapescript 36a

a I was only twelve years old when my mother died and I started work.
b I was always tired in my first job because I

worked very long hours.
c I started work at 5.30 in the morning and I finished at 9.00 in the evening.
d Now I live in a village, but in 1920 I lived in London.
e Now I look after my five cats. In the 1920s I looked after five children.
f I loved all the children, but I loved Robert especially.
g Robert's over seventy now and I still see him. He visited me just last month.

Tapescript 36b

worked	lived	died	started	loved
finished	looked	visited	cleaned	liked
stayed	moved			

Tapescript 37

Where was she born?
When did she die?
When did her father die?
When did she marry Prince Albert?
Where did they live?
How many children did they have?

Tapescript 38

had	came	worked	went
left	hated	got	gave
became	wrote	changed	won
lost	found	bought	sold

Tapescript 39

What can I remember? Well, I left school in 1982. I was unemployed for two years, but then I found a job in an office. I sold computer software to businesses.
Suddenly computers were everywhere! Banks, hotels, hospitals, schools, homes. My Mum and Dad bought a video recorder in 1985, and my little brother got a computer video game for his birthday in 1986.
Near the end of the 1980s things got worse and in 1990 I lost my job.
Now, sport. Well, in 1980 the United States didn't go to the Olympics in Moscow, and in 1984 the USSR didn't go to the Olympics in Los Angeles, but they both went to Seoul in 1988.
Argentina won the World Cup in 1986, and Germany won it in 1990.
What about politics? Well, Mrs Thatcher was our Prime Minister for the whole of the 1980s. Reagan became the US president in 1981, Gorbachev gave the world *glasnost* and *perestroika*, and the Berlin Wall came down in 1989. Then all sorts of things changed.

Tapescript 40a

a walk   d writer   g work   j half
b listen   e autumn   h short   k foreign
c know   f farm   i high   l daughter

Tapescript 40b

a talk   f white
b born   g knife
c bought   h wrong
d world   i cupboard
e answer   j Christmas

Tapescript 41a

a A Ugh! Work again! I hate Mondays!
  B Me too. Did you have a nice weekend?
  A Yes. It was wonderful.

b Happy birthday to you.
  Happy birthday to you.
  Happy birthday, dear Katie.
  Happy birthday to you.

c A How many Easter eggs did you get?
  B Six. What about you?
  A Five. I had them all on Easter morning before lunch.
  B Did you?
  A And then I was sick!
  B Ugh!

d A Congratulations!
  B Oh ... thank you very much.
  A When's the happy day?
  B Pardon?
  A Your wedding day. When is it?
  B Oh! We're not sure yet. Some time in June, probably.

e A Hello! Merry Christmas, everyone!
  B Merry Christmas! Come in, come in. It's so cold outside.

f A Wonderful! It's Friday!
  B Yes. Have a nice weekend!
  A Same to you.

Tapescript 41b

a Did you have a nice weekend?
b Happy birthday!
c Merry Christmas!
d Have a nice weekend!
e Congratulations!

UNIT 8

Tapescript 42

The hamburger
An American chef from Connecticut, Louis Lassen, made and sold the first hamburgers in 1895. He called them hamburgers because sailors from Hamburg in Germany gave him the recipe. Students from Yale University and businessmen loved them and bought them. Kenneth Lassen, Louis' grandson still sells hamburgers in Connecticut.

Television
A Scotsman, John Logie Baird, transmitted the first television picture on 25 October, 1925. The first person on television was a boy who worked in the office next to Baird's workroom in London.
In 1927 Baird sent pictures from London to Glasgow. In 1928 he sent pictures to New York and also produced the first colour TV pictures.

The ball-point pen
A Hungarian, Laszlo Biro, made the first ball-point pen in 1938. In 1944 the British Army bought thirty thousand because soldiers could write with them outside in the rain. At the end of the war 'Biros' quickly became very popular all over the world. In 1948 a shop in New York sold ten thousand on one day.

Tapescript 43

A Did you know that Marco Polo brought spaghetti back from China?
B Really? He didn't! That's incredible!
A Well, it's true!

A Did you know that Napoleon was afraid of cats?
B He wasn't! I don't believe it!
A Well, it's true!

Tapescript 44

On 1 June 1992 a French burglar broke into a house in Paris. He went into the living room and stole two pictures. Then he went into the kitchen. He opened the fridge and saw some cheese. He was hungry, so he ate all the cheese. Next he saw two bottles of champagne. He was very thirsty, so he drank both bottles. Then he felt sleepy. He went upstairs for a rest, but he was tired and he fell asleep. When he woke up the next morning, there were four policemen around the bed.

Tapescript 45

Wendy Mint

Well, it was five years ago. A Sunday evening five years ago. I was in the bath and the radio was on. Er ... I always listen to pop music in the bath. Suddenly I heard this voice, the disc jockey's voice. It was beautiful, really beautiful. Warm and friendly. I thought, 'Oh! What a lovely voice!' I think I fell in love then, with his voice. Well, I listened to the end of the programme and I heard his name, Oliver Mint. I loved the name, too.
Well, er ... usually I'm quite shy, but this time I wasn't. I went to the telephone and I rang the radio station. I couldn't believe it! Suddenly there was his voice on the telephone! And we talked and talked, for about half an hour. And he said, 'Where do you live?' so I told him, and then he said, 'Can we meet?' And I said 'Yes, please!' So we met in an Italian restaurant the next evening. I was so nervous, but it was wonderful! We got married a month later and now we have a lovely baby boy. He's nearly two!

Trevor Richards

Well, I have a baker's shop. I make all the bread and cakes for it. And one day ... it was a very hot day in summer, er ... the summer of 1976, and it was lunchtime and er ... this beautiful girl came into the shop. She was with some friends and I could hear that they weren't English, but they spoke English very well and er ... they all bought sandwiches and went to the park. Well, I couldn't forget her. The way she smiled, the way she laughed, her blue, blue eyes. I waited and watched every lunchtime but she didn't come back into the shop.
Then suddenly, there she was again, and so I said, 'Hello again. You're still in England, then?' And she said, 'Yes. But this is my last day. I go back to Sweden tomorrow.' And she smiled. Now, usually I'm shy, but I took a small pink cake and I wrote *I love you* on it. And when she asked for a chicken sandwich, I looked into the blue, blue eyes and I gave her the cake! She laughed and said, 'I didn't know English men were so romantic!' Well, after that she went back to Sweden, but we wrote letters and in 1978 we got married. Now we work together in the shop and we have three children.

Tapescript 46a

first   second   third   fourth   fifth
sixth   tenth   twelfth   thirteenth
sixteenth   seventeenth   twentieth
twenty-first   thirtieth   thirty-first

Tapescript 46b

the first of April   April the first
the second of March   March the second
the sevententh of September   September the seventeenth
the nineteenth of November   November the nineteenth
the twenty-third of June   June the twenty-third
the fifteenth of July, nineteen sixty-seven
the twenty-ninth of February, nineteen seventy-six
the nineteenth of December, nineteen eighty-three
the third of October, nineteen seventy
the thirty-first of May, nineteen ninety-three

Tapescript 46c

1   The fourth of January
2   May the seventh, nineteen twenty-two
3   The thirtieth of August, nineteen sixty-five
4   A   It was Friday. I know it was Friday!
    B   No, it wasn't. It was Saturday!
    A   No. I remember. It was Friday the thirteenth. The thirteenth of October!
5   A   Oh no! I forgot your birthday.
    B   It doesn't matter, really.
    A   It was last Sunday, the second. June the second. Oh I am sorry!
6   A   Hey! Did you know this? Shakespeare was born and died on the same day!
    B   That's not possible!
    A   Yes, it is. He was born on April the twenty-third, fifteen sixty-four and he died on April the twenty-third, sixteen sixteen!

Word list

Here is a list of some of the words from the units of *Headway Elementary*.
Write the translation.

adj = adjective
adv = adverb
conj= conjunction
opp = opposite
pl = plural
prep = preposition
pron = pronoun
pp = past participle
n = noun
v = verb

UNIT 1

and (*conj*) /ənd/
apple (*n*) /æpl/
bag (*n*) /bæg/
brother (*n*) /brʌðə(r)/
camera (*n*) /kæmrə/
child (*n*) (*pl* children) /tʃaɪld/
country (*n*) /kʌntrɪ/
daughter (*n*) /dɔ:tə(r)/
dictionary (*n*) /dɪkʃənrɪ/
doctor (*n*) /dɒktə(r)/
envelope (*n*) /envələʊp/
evening (*n*) /i:vnɪŋ/
first (*adj*) /fɜ:st/
flat (*n*) /flæt/
have (*v*) /hæv/
house (*n*) /haʊs/
international (*adj*) /ɪntənæʃənl/
job (*n*) /dʒɒb/
key (*n*) /ki:/
language (*n*) /læŋgwɪdʒ/
learn (*v*) /lɜ:n/
letter (*n*) /letə(r)/
live (*v*) /lɪv/
magazine (*n*) /mægəzi:n/
map (*n*) /mæp/
married (*adj*) /mærɪd/
name (*n*) /neɪm/
newspaper (*n*) /nju:speɪpə(r)/
notebook (*n*) /nəʊtbʊk/
orange (*n*) /ɒrɪndʒ/
people (*n*) /pi:pl/
postcard (*n*) /pəʊstka:d/
sister (*n*) /sɪstə(r)/
son (*n*) /sʌn/
south (*n*) /saʊθ/
stamp (*n*) /stæmp/
student (*n*) /stju:dənt/
suitcase (*n*) /su:tkeɪs/
surname (*n*) /sɜ:neɪm/

teacher (*n*) /ti:tʃə(r)/
thank you/thanks /θæŋk ju:, θæŋks/
ticket (*n*) /tɪkɪt/
want (*v*) /wɒnt/

UNIT 2

address (*n*) /ədres/
aunt (*n*) /a:nt/
beautiful (*adj*) /bju:tɪfl/
big (*adj*) /bɪg/
book (*n*) /bʊk/
boyfriend (*n*) /bɔɪfrend/
cheap (*adj*) /tʃi:p/
cheese (*n*) /tʃi:z/
chicken (*n*) /tʃɪkɪn/
coffee (*n*) /kɒfɪ/
cold (*adj*) /kəʊld/
cup (*n*) /kʌp/
difficult (*adj*) /dɪfɪkəlt/
drink (*v*) /drɪŋk/
easy (*adj*) /i:zɪ/
expensive (*adj*) /ɪkspensɪv/
family (*n*) /fæməlɪ/
father (*n*) /fa:ðə(r)/
food (*n*) /fu:d/
friendly (*adj*) /frendlɪ/
good (*adj*) /gʊd/
grandfather (*n*) /grændfa:ðə(r)/
grandmother (*n*) /grændmʌðə(r)/
ham (*n*) /hæm/
happy (*adj*) /hæpɪ/
holiday (*n*) /hɒlɪdeɪ/
home (*n*) (at home) /həʊm/
horrible (*adj*) /hɒrəbl/
hot (*adj*) /hɒt/
husband (*n*) /hʌzbənd/
ice-cream (*n*) /aɪs kri:m/
lovely (*adj*) /lʌvlɪ/
milk (*n*) /mɪlk/
mineral water (*n*) /mɪnərəl wɔ:tə(r)/
morning (*n*) /mɔ:nɪŋ/
mother (*n*) /mʌðə(r)/
nephew (*n*) /nefju:/
new (*adj*) /nju:/
nice (*adj*) /naɪs/
niece (*n*) /ni:s/
old (*adj*) /əʊld/
or (*conj*) /ɔ:(r)/
orange juice (*n*) /ɒrɪndʒ dʒu:s/
parents (*n*) /peərənts/
park (*n*) /pa:k/
phone number (*n*) /fəʊn nʌmbə(r)/
photo (*n*) /fəʊtəʊ/
right (*adj*) (*opp* wrong) /raɪt/
sandwich (*n*) /sænwɪdʒ/
small (*adj*) /smɔ:l/

tea (*n*) /ti:/
today (*adv*) /tədeɪ/
town (*n*) /taʊn/
uncle (*n*) /ʌŋkl/
understand (*v*) /ʌndəstænd/
weather (*n*) /weðə(r)/
wife (*n*) /waɪf/
work (*n*) (at work) /wɜ:k/
write (*v*) /raɪt/
wrong (*adj*) /rɒŋ/
young (*adj*) /jʌŋ/

UNIT 3

actor (*n*) /æktə(r)/
afternoon (*n*) /a:ftənu:n/
arrive (*v*) /əraɪv/
baker (*n*) /beɪkə(r)/
because (*conj*) /bɪkɒz/
bread (*n*) /bred/
but (*conj*) /bʌt/
car (*n*) /ka:(r)/
catch (*v*) (catch a train) /kætʃ/
certainly (*adv*) /sɜ:tənlɪ/
come (*v*) /kʌm/
cost (*v*) /kɒst/
drive (*v*) /draɪv/
evening (*n*) /i:vnɪŋ/
film (*n*) /fɪlm/
fly (*v*) /flaɪ/
football (*n*) /fʊtbɔ:l/
fortunately (*adv*) /fɔ:tʃənətlɪ/
go (*v*) /gəʊ/
hairdresser (*n*) /heədresə(r)/
half (*n*) /ha:f/
hospital (*n*) /hɒspɪtl/
hour (*n*) /aʊə(r)/
interpreter (*n*) /ɪntɜ:prɪtə(r)/
journalist (*n*) /dʒɜ:nəlɪst/
journey (*n*) /dʒɜ:nɪ/
leave (*v*) /li:v/
like (*v*) /laɪk/
look after (*v*) /lʊk a:ftə(r)/
love (*v*) /lʌv/
make (*v*) /meɪk/
mechanic (*n*) /məkænɪk/
mend (*v*) /mend/
mountain (*n*) /maʊntɪn/
nurse (*n*) /nɜ:s/
pilot (*n*) /paɪlət/
plane (*n*) /pleɪn/
play (*v*) /pleɪ/
receptionist (*n*) /rɪsepʃənɪst/
sea (*n*) /si:/
see (*v*) /si:/
sell (*v*) /sel/

shop (*n*) /ʃɒp/
shop assistant (*n*) /ʃɒp əsɪstənt/
singer (*n*) /sɪŋə(r)/
speak (*v*) /spi:k/
summer (*n*) /sʌmə(r)/
take (*v*) /teɪk/
taxi-driver (*n*) /tæksɪ draɪvə(r)/
teach (*v*) /ti:tʃ/
tired (*adj*) /taɪəd/
train (*n*) /treɪn/
village (*n*) /vɪlɪdʒ/
walk (*v*) /wɔ:k/
week (*n*) /wi:k/
winter (*n*) /wɪntə(r)/

UNIT 4

autumn (*n*) /ɔ:təm/
bad (*adj*) /bæd/
baseball (*n*) /beɪsbɔ:l/
beach (*n*) /bi:tʃ/
bed (*n*) /bed/
bring (*v*) /brɪŋ/
brown (*adj*) /braʊn/
cards (*n*) (play cards) /ka:dz/
chat (*v*) /tʃæt/
colour (*n*) /kʌlə(r)/
computer (*n*) /kəmpju:tə(r)/
cook (*v*) /kʊk/
crossword (*n*) /krɒswɜ:d/
dance (*v*) /da:ns/
dinner (*n*) /dɪnə(r)/
eat (*v*) /i:t/
exciting (*adj*) /ɪksaɪtɪŋ/
exercise (*n*) (do exercise) /eksəsaɪz/
favourite (*adj*) /feɪvərɪt/
fish (*n*) /fɪʃ/
flower (*n*) /flaʊə(r)/
friend (*n*) /frend/
game (*n*) /geɪm/
get up (*v*) /get ʌp/
go shopping (*v*) /gəʊ ʃɒpɪŋ/
go swimming (*v*) /gəʊ swɪmɪŋ/
here (*adv*) /hɪə(r)/
hobby (*n*) /hɒbɪ/
ice-skating (*n*) /aɪs skeɪtɪŋ/
interesting (*adj*) /ɪntrəstɪŋ/
interview (*v*) /ɪntəvju:/
know (*v*) /nəʊ/
late (*adv*) /leɪt/
listen to (*v*) /lɪsən tu:, tə/
long (*adj*) /lɒŋ/
meet (*v*) /mi:t/
month (*n*) /mʌnθ/
near (*prep*) /nɪə(r)/
never (*adv*) /nevə(r)/

office (n) /ɒfɪs/
often (adv) /ɒfn, ɒftən/
painting (n) /peɪntɪŋ/
pub (n) /pʌb/

red (adj) /red/
relax (v) /rɪlæks/
river (n) /rɪvə(r)/

sailing (n) /seɪlɪŋ/
short (adj) /ʃɔ:t/
smoke (v) /sməʊk/
sometimes (adv) /sʌmtaɪmz/
song (n) /sɒŋ/
spring (n) /sprɪŋ/
start (v) /stɑ:t/
stay (v) /steɪ/
suddenly (adv) /sʌdənlɪ/
summer (n) /sʌmə(r)/
sunbathe (v) /sʌnbeɪð/

take photographs (v) /teɪk fəʊtəgrɑ:fs/
traffic (n) /træfɪk/
tree (n) /tri:/

usually (adv) /ju:ʒəlɪ/

visit (v) /vɪzɪt/
volleyball (n) /vɒlɪbɔ:l/

watch (v) /wɒtʃ/
wet (adj) /wet/
windsurf (v) /wɪndsɜ:f/

yellow (adj) /jeləʊ/

UNIT 5

also (adj) /ɔ:lsəʊ/
armchair (n) /ɑ:mtʃeə(r)/

bath (n) /bɑ:θ/
bathroom (n) /bɑ:θru:m/
bedroom (n) /bedru:m/
behind (prep) /bɪhaɪnd/

carpet (n) /kɑ:pɪt/
chemist's (n) /kemɪsts/
clean (adj) /kli:n/
clock (n) /klɒk/
clothes (n) /kləʊðz/
cooker (n) /kʊkə(r)/
cupboard (n) /kʌbəd/

desk (n) /desk/
dishwasher (n) /dɪʃwɒʃə(r)/
dog (n) /dɒg/
during (prep) /djʊərɪŋ/

everybody (pron) /evrɪbɒdɪ/

famous (adj) /feɪməs/
fire (n) /faɪə(r)/
fridge (n) /frɪdʒ/

garden (n) /gɑ:dn/

important (adj) /ɪmpɔ:tənt/
in front of (prep) /ɪn frʌnt əv/

king (n) /kɪŋ/
kitchen (n) /kɪtʃɪn/

lamp (n) /læmp/
left (adv) (opp right) /left/
library (n) /laɪbrərɪ/
like (prep) /laɪk/
living room (n) /lɪvɪŋ ru:m/

meal (n) /mi:l/
mirror (n) /mɪrə(r)/
modern (adj) /mɒdn/

news (n) /nju:z/
newsagent's (n) /nju:zeɪdʒənts/
next to (prep) /nekst tu:, tə/

on (prep) /ɒn/
other (adj) /ʌðə(r)/

palace (n) /pælɪs/
pen (n) /pen/
picture (n) /pɪktʃə(r)/
place (n) /pleɪs/
plant (n) /plɑ:nt/
plate (n) /pleɪt/
police station (n) /pəli:s steɪʃn/
politician (n) /pɒlətɪʃn/
post box (n) /pəʊst bɒx/
post office (n) /pəʊst ɒfɪs/
radio (n) /reɪdɪəʊ/
right (adv) (opp left) /raɪt/

sleep (v) /sli:p/
sofa (n) /səʊfə(r)/
stereo (n) /sterɪəʊ/
swimming pool (n) /swɪmɪŋ pu:l/

table (n) /teɪbl/
talk (v) /tɔ:k/
toilet (n) /tɔɪlət/

wall (n) /wɔ:l/
washing machine (n) /wɒʃɪŋ məʃi:n/
while (conj) /waɪl/
whole (adj) /həʊl/
window (n) /wɪndəʊ/

UNIT 6

again (adv) /əgen, əgeɪn/
arrival hall (n) /əraɪvəl hɔ:l/

baggage reclaim (n) /bægɪdʒ ri:kleɪm/
bike (n) /baɪk/
black (adj) /blæk/
boarding pass (n) /bɔ:dɪŋ pɑ:s/
boring (adj) /bɔ:rɪŋ/
(be) born (v) /bɔ:n/
brilliant (adj) /brɪlɪənt/

champion (n) /tʃæmpɪən/
check (v) /tʃek/
check-in desk (n) /tʃek ɪn desk/
cheque (n) /tʃek/
chess (n) /tʃes/
count (v) /kaʊnt/

conversation (n) /kɒnvəseɪʃn/
dark (adj) /dɑ:k/
delayed (pp) (be delayed) /dɪleɪd/
departure lounge (n) /dɪpɑ:tʃə laʊndʒ/
destination (n) /destɪneɪʃn/
different (adj) /dɪfrənt/
draw (v) /drɔ:/
eye (n) /aɪ/

flight (n) /flaɪt/
fluently (adv) /flu:əntlɪ/

gate (n) (airport) /geɪt/
genius (n) /dʒi:nɪəs/

hand luggage (n) /hænd lʌgɪdʒ/
hear (v) /hɪə(r)/

land (v) /lænd/
last (adj) (last month/year) /lɑ:st/
lunch (n) /lʌntʃ/

match (n) (football) /mætʃ/
meat (n) /mi:t/
medicine (n) (study medicine) /medsn/

nose (n) /nəʊz/
now (adv) /naʊ/

party (n) /pɑ:tɪ/
passport control (n) /pɑ:spɔ:t kəntrəʊl/
piano (n) /pɪænəʊ/
player (n) /pleɪə(r)/
practise (v) /præktɪs/

ride (v) /raɪd/

safety belt (n) /seɪftɪ belt/
smell (v) /smel/
study (v) /stʌdɪ/

teenager (n) /ti:neɪdʒə(r)/
think (v) /θɪŋk/
translate (v) /trænzleɪt/
tray (n) /treɪ/
type (v) /taɪp/

under (prep) (under 18 years old) /ʌndə(r)/
until (conj) (not until) /ʌntɪl/
use (v) /ju:z/

wear (v) /weə(r)/

year (n) /jɪə(r)/
yesterday (adv) /jestədeɪ/

UNIT 7

abroad (adv) /əbrɔ:d/

baby (n) /beɪbɪ/
become (v) /bɪkʌm/
before (prep) /bɪfɔ:(r)/
borrow (v) /bɒrəʊ/
bottle (n) /bɒtl/
buy (v) /baɪ/

change (v) /tʃeɪndʒ/
character (n) /kærɪktə(r)/

Christmas (n) /krɪsməs/
clean (v) /kli:n/
clerk (n) /klɑ:k/
debt (n) /det/
description (n) /dɪskrɪpʃn/
die (v) /daɪ/

earn (v) /ɜ:n/
Easter (n) /i:stə(r)/
enjoy (v) /ɪndʒɔɪ/
especially (adv) /ɪspeʃəlɪ/
experience (n) /ɪkspɪərɪəns/

factory (n) /fæktərɪ/
find (v) /faɪnd/
finish (v) /fɪnɪʃ/

get (v) (= receive, become) /get/
give (v) /gɪv/
great (adj) (writer) /greɪt/

hard (adj) (life) /hɑ:d/
hate (v) /heɪt/

immediately (adv) /ɪmi:dɪətlɪ/

kiss (v) /kɪs/

later (adv) /leɪtə(r)/
life (n) /laɪf/
lose (v) /lu:z/

marry (v) /mærɪ/
move (v) /mu:v/

night (n) /naɪt/
novel (n) /nɒvəl/
novelist (n) /nɒvəlɪst/

over (prep) (over 90 years old) /əʊvə(r)/

past (n) /pɑ:st/
politics (n) /pɒlətɪks/
poor (adj) /pʊə(r), pɔ:(r)/
popular (adj) /pɒpjʊlə(r)/
present (n) /prezənt/
pretty (adj) /prɪtɪ/
prison (n) /prɪzn/
probably (adv) /prɒbəblɪ/

real (adj) /rɪəl/
remember (v) /rɪmembə(r)/
retire (v) /rɪtaɪə(r)/
rich (adj) /rɪtʃ/

sell (v) /sel/
send (v) /send/
software (n) /sɒftweə(r)/
spend (v) /spend/
still (adv) /stɪl/
successful (adj) /səksesfəl/
suddenly (adv) /sʌdənlɪ/

tomorrow (adv) /təmɒrəʊ/

unemployed (adj) /ʌnɪmplɔɪd/

video recorder (n) /vɪdɪəʊ rɪkɔ:də(r)/

war (n) /wɔ:(r)/
wedding (n) /wedɪŋ/
win (v) /wɪn/
wonderful (adj) /wʌndəfəl/

UNIT 8

actress (n) /ˈæktrəs/
afraid (adj) (afraid of)
  /əˈfreɪd əv/
alive (adj) /əˈlaɪv/
angry (adj) /ˈæŋgrɪ/
around (prep) /əˈraʊnd/
asleep (adj) /əˈsliːp/

baker (n) /ˈbeɪkə(r)/
believe (v) /bɪˈliːv/
birthday (n) /ˈbɜːθdeɪ/
biscuit (n) /ˈbɪskɪt/
blue (adj) /bluː/
burglar (n) /ˈbɜːglə(r)/
businessman/woman (n)
  /ˈbɪznɪsmən,
  ˈbɪznɪswʊmən/

cake (n) /keɪk/
call (v) (name) /kɔːl/
call (n) (telephone) /kɔːl/
century (n) /ˈsentʃərɪ/
chef (n) /ʃef/
couple (n) /ˈkʌpl/
cousin (n) /ˈkʌzən/

date (n) /deɪt/
disc jockey (n)
  /ˈdɪsk dʒɒkɪ/

engaged (v) (get engaged)
  /ɪŋˈgeɪdʒd/
exam (n) /ɪgˈzæm/

fall asleep (v)
  /fɔːl əˈsliːp/
fall in love (v)
  /fɔːl ɪn lʌv/
feel (v) /fiːl/

hair (n) /heə(r)/
hamburger (n)
  /ˈhæmbɜːgə(r)/
hard (adv) (work hard)
  /hɑːd/
hungry (adj) /ˈhʌŋgrɪ/

incredible (adj) /ɪnˈkredəbl/

jeans (n) /dʒiːnz/
joke (n) /dʒəʊk/

laugh (v) /lɑːf, læf/

nervous (adj) /ˈnɜːvəs/

pink (adj) /pɪŋk/
policeman (n) /pəˈliːsmən/
produce (v) /prəˈdʒuːs/

quickly (adv) /ˈkwɪklɪ/

rain (n) /reɪn/
really (adv) /ˈrɪəlɪ/
recipe (n) /ˈresəpɪ/
record (n) (music)
  /ˈrekɔːd/
rest (n) (have a rest)
  /rest/
ring (v) (telephone) /rɪŋ/
romantic (adj)
  /rəʊˈmæntɪk/

sailor (n) /ˈseɪlə(r)/
same (adj) /seɪm/
say (v) /seɪ/
season (n) /ˈsiːzn/
shy (adj) /ʃaɪ/

sleepy (adj) /ˈsliːpɪ/
smile (v) /smaɪl/
snow (v) /snəʊ/
soldier (n) /ˈsəʊldʒə(r)/
steal (v) /stiːl/

tell (v) /tel/
together (adv) /təˈgeðə(r)/
travel (v) /ˈtrævl/
typewriter (n)
  /ˈtaɪpraɪtə(r)/

upstairs (adv) /ʌpˈsteəz/

voice (n) /vɔɪs/

wake up (v) /weɪk ʌp/
wait (v) /weɪt/
warm (adj) /wɔːm/

Appendix 1

IRREGULAR VERBS

Base form	Past Simple	Past Participle
be	was/were	been
become	became	become
begin	began	begun
break	broke	broken
bring	brought	brought
build	built	built
buy	bought	bought
can	could	been able
catch	caught	caught
choose	chose	chosen
come	came	come
cost	cost	cost
cut	cut	cut
do	did	done
drink	drank	drunk
drive	drove	driven
eat	ate	eaten
fall	fell	fallen
feel	felt	felt
fight	fought	fought
find	found	found
fly	flew	flown
forget	forgot	forgotten
get	got	got
give	gave	given
go	went	gone/been
grow	grew	grown
have	had	had
hear	heard	heard
hit	hit	hit
keep	kept	kept
know	knew	known
learn	learnt/learned	learnt/learned
leave	left	left
lose	lost	lost
make	made	made
meet	met	met
pay	paid	paid
put	put	put
read /ri:d/	read /red/	read /red/
ride	rode	ridden
run	ran	run
say	said	said
see	saw	seen
sell	sold	sold
send	sent	sent
shut	shut	shut
sing	sang	sung
sit	sat	sat
sleep	slept	slept
speak	spoke	spoken
spend	spent	spent
stand	stood	stood
steal	stole	stolen
swim	swam	swum
take	took	taken
tell	told	told
think	thought	thought
understand	understood	understood
wake	woke	woken
wear	wore	worn
win	won	won
write	wrote	written

Appendix 2

VERB PATTERNS

Verb + *-ing*	
like love enjoy hate finish stop	swimming cooking

Verb + *to* + infinitive	
choose decide forget promise need help hope try want would like would love	to go to work

Note

Have to for obligation is followed by the infinitive.

    I have to go now. Goodbye.

Verb + *-ing* or *to* + infintive	
begin start	raining/to rain

Modal auxiliary verbs	
can could shall will would	go arrive